Fighting Co

CW00394493

CENTURY SERIES

in Color

by Lou Drendel

squadron/signal publications

ISBN 0-89747-097-4

If you have any photographs of the aircraft, armor, soldiers or ships of any nation, particularly wartime snapshots, why not share them with us and help make Squadron/Signal's books all the more interesting and complete in the future. Any photograph sent to us will be copied and the original returned. The donor will be fully credited for any photos used. Please send them to: Squadron/Signal Publications, Inc., 1115 Crowley Dr., Carrollton, TX 75006.

Federal Standard Color Equivalents

(as listed in FS 595a)

Insignia Blue 15044
Insignia White 17875
Insignia Red 11136
Gloss Black 17038
Black 37038
International Orange 12197
Dark Green 34079
Undersurface Gray 36622
Tan 20400
Brown 30140
Tan (more Brown than 20400) 30219
Green, Olive Drab 34102

| Brown 30140 | Tan 20400 | Tan 30219 | Gray 36622 |

| Dark Green 34079 | Green, OD 34102 | Natural Metal | Int. Orange 12197 |

Introduction

When Chuck Yeager blasted through the sound barrier in **Glamorous Glennis,** the Bell X-1, on October 14, 1947, it was the beginning of a technological revolution. Until Yeager proved that the sound barrier was no barrier at all, it was a widely held belief that the speed of sound ended in a solid wall, an impenetrable obstruction that would mash anything that attempted to traverse its forbidden corridors. Crossing that threshold opened new vistas for aircraft designers and tacticians alike. They were quick to explore those vistas. Within ten years a whole new family of American military aircraft were routinely flying supersonic missions. This is a pictorial survey of one branch of that family, the so-called "Century Series" of USAF fighters, which is popularly acknowledged to include the F-100 through the F-106, and perhaps to a purist or two, even the F-107 and F-110.

The Century Series is more than just a collection of airplanes to those of us who lived through that time. It is an embodiment of American military and, perhaps even public, thinking during the 'fifties.

The 'fifties were a golden decade for American military aviation. The cold war was on and, even if you didn't think it would turn hot anytime soon, you didn't question the necessity to be ready...just in case. (Pearl Harbor was fresh enough in everyone's mind and just about every American who had attained the age of reason could remember the result of too much isolationism.) Korea had proven that there were still dragons to be slain. It had also proven that the Russians were more than just a bunch of ignorant Cossacks when it came to designing jet fighters. They couldn't begin to compete when it came to flying fighters, but the MiG 15 proved they knew how to build them. Curtis LeMay was spared the fate of Billy Mitchell. The

public believed, and Congress funded. The USAF became the mightiest military organization the world had ever seen.

The Century Series reflected diverse design philosphies and tactical requirements. It was a showcase for American design genius, which might well be characterized as one of our "great leaps forward". The Century Series continues to soldier on into the 'eighties, but they were born in the 'fifties. In my mind they will always recall those days when American Airpower was unchallenged qualitatively and quantitatively.

My friend Dave Menard suggested that this book might better be titled "Century Series, B.C. (Before Camouflage)". Indeed, many of the series were at their esthetic best before camouflage came into vogue in the mid-'sixties. The application of camouflage was more than just another attempt at the age old brass hat dream of imposing total uniformity upon their troops....particularly the more spirited and innovative troops....the fighter pilots. It was a precursor of dreary days to come for the Century Series. It was tacit acknowledgement that we needed visual deception to accomplish our mission. The gaudy squadron markings which adorned the Century Series in the 'fifties and 'sixties were more than just decoration. They spoke (and sometimes shouted) of a unit's *esprit de corps.* They proclaimed to the world; "Here we come and we don't care how easy it is for you to see us, for we are invincible!" We won't ignore camouflage in this book.....it is a part of the story of the Century Series.....but we will try to concentrate on the *joie de vivre* of those gloriously colorful days "B.C." This then, is a nostalgia book. The stage is set. Return with us now to those halcyon days of yesteryear, when out of the west there echoed the thundering roar of J-57s and J-75s...............

F-100A-5-NA of the Wright Air Development Center, Wright-Patterson AFB, in 1953. The characteristic discoloration of the aft fuselage is caused by the reaction of the titanium alloy to heat. F-100 was the first aircraft to employ large amounts of titanium. North American purchased over 80% of all titanium produced in the U.S. in 1953 and 1954. (Peter Bowers via Jim Sullivan.)

F-100 Super Sabre

It was one thing to prove that you could fly faster than the speed of sound in an experimental rocket-powered research aircraft. The real trick was coming up with an airplane that could do it on a day-to-day basis, with a reliable turbojet engine. Much is made of the genius of aircraft designers, while a lot less is made of the contributions of the powerplant designers who really provide the heart and soul of an aircraft. (There can be advantages to this too. When the F-111 got into big trouble because of engine problems, the press never said; "A Pratt & Whitney TF-30 crashed while attached to an F-111.")

While North American Aviation had made a commitment to producing a supersonic fighter in the late '40s and was backing it up with corporate funds, Pratt & Whitney had also made a commitment. P&W was determined to become the engine supplier to the aerospace industry. There was no question that the jet was the engine of the future and P&W hit upon the idea of a split compressor turbine, which solved many of the most vexing performance problems being encountered with jet engines. By 1950 the J-57 had emerged as a viable concept with 9,250 lbs. thrust in mil power and 14,000 lbs. in afterburner being promised. North American had found the engine around which to design the F-100.

In those pre-Korea days, the newly created USAF was less than convinced of the immediate need for a supersonic fighter and showed little interest in North American's proposals. Attitudes were rotated 180 degrees when the first MiG-15s were encountered, though, and NAA began to receive strong official encouragement. That encouragement soon became an order for two prototypes in November 1951. The F-100 was officially born and the Century Series was launched.

The first **YF-100** made its debut on May 25, 1953 with company test pilot George Welch at the controls. Welch had finished his tour of WWII Army Air Force duty as an 18½ kill ace, the first four kills being scored over Oahu on December 7, 1941. Twelve years later Welch accomplished another first as he took the YF-100 through the sound barrier on its first flight....in level flight. It was the first turbojet-powered aircraft to do so.

If the Air Force had been somewhat reluctant to jump with both feet into the supersonic fighter business in the late 'forties, they were now more impatient than a middle-aged bride. NAA testing of much of the flight envelope and systems was completed within the

F-100C-5-NAs of the 450th Fighter Day Group, Foster AFB, Texas in 1956 markings, with red scalloped nose flash. The 322nd Group pioneered trans-Atlantic non-stop deployments in the 1956 exercise "Mobile Baker", flying from Foster to Sidi Slimane, Morocco, then on to Landstuhl, Germany. (Peter Bowers via Jim Sullivan)

first 100 flight hours, which occured within six weeks of that first flight. The Air Force test pilots, headed by Pete Everest, began flying the F-100 in July and by September the Phase II flight testing was completed. The second prototype was rolled out and flown on October 14. In the meantime, tooling for production F-100As had proceeded. The first A model came off the line and was flown on October 29. The A model incorporated what seemed a minor change at the time. Its vertical fin and rudder were shortened in an effort to cut down drag and weight. This change was to have a catastrophic consequence.

During the test program, the Air Force allowed orientation flights by fighter pilots other than test pilots. The nearly unanimous reaction of all of them was an unqualified "gee whiz!" Practically the only serious dissenter was Pete Everest, who was not at all convinced of the F-100's stability out at those ragged edges where much of the serious business of fighter pilots is conducted. Welch himself thought the airplane was just fine. The Air Force was in no mood for any dilly-dallying when it came to getting their hot new fighter into the operational inventory.

By the end of September 1954, 60 A models had come off the production line and the 479th Day Fighter Wing was activated at George AFB, California. On October 14, George Welch took off on his last test flight. The mission that day was to dive the airplane to its limiting

F-100A-20-NA of the Arizona Air Guard at Phoenix, 1962. Markings are yellow edged in black. (Paul Stevens)

F-100C-25-NA Immediately after delivery to George AFB, California. A total of 451 of the C model were built before production was switched to the D in 1956. The F-100C was the fastest of all Super Sabres, with an officially listed top speed of 924 mph at 35,000 feet. (North American)

Mach number, then pull the max design load limit (7½ G) on pull-out. Some nagging doubts had cropped up, as there had been four cases of F-100s coming apart in flight in the preceding few months. At 11AM Welch began his fatal dive, aiming his Super Sabre at Rosamond Dry Lake. The dive was begun at 45,000 feet. Shortly after passing through 25,000 feet, the F-100 exploded. Though Welch ejected, or was ejected, he died before reaching the ground. All production F-100s were grounded while NAA began an intensive investigation. Since this had been a specially instrumented aircraft, some clues to what had happened remained. Specifically, there was film from a camera mounted in the vertical fin, aimed at the left tailplane. A long and complex technical explanation can be shortened by simply saying that Everest had been right. The F-100 lacked directional stability at high Mach and high G loadings.

All F-100s on the production line were modified with a larger fin and rudder, and 27 inches were added to wingspan. Operational F-100s were retrofitted with these modifications. Production and squadron introduction of the Super Sabre continued.

The Super Sabre was to TAC what your first new car was to you. It was the single most important worldwide "show the flag" instrument we had in the mid to late 'fifties. It pioneered aerial refuelling on a routine basis for overseas deployment, the boom of a J-57 afterburner lighting off could be heard from Sidi Slimane to Itazuke. By mid-1957 TAC had 16 wings of F-100s and the following year the Air National Guard received its first F-100As as the 188th TFS of the New Mexico Guard checked out in the Super Sabre. By that time the Hun had undergone the metamorphosis of shedding its day fighter role for that of an all-weather fighter-bomber.

Even before the F-100A became operational, the **F-100C** had been authorized. (The **F-100B** was to have been an all-weather interceptor, and evolved into the F-107) The F-100C was the first of the bomber models of the Hun. As such, it incorporated the following changes from the A; strengthened wing with six hardpoints for ordnance or fuel tanks, increased fuel capacity (from 744 to 1702 gallons), uprated J-57 engine (10,200 lbs. dry and 16,950 lbs. with afterburner), MA-2 LABS (Low Altitude Bombing System) for delivery of nuclear weapons and an aerial refuelling system. The initial C models were the last 70 As scheduled for production. The C made its maiden flight on January 17, 1955. It set a two-run speed record of 822 mph on August 20 and was in the hands of the first unit to operate the "C", the 322nd Fighter Day Group, at Foster AFB, Texas that same month.

Also in the works was a two seat version, which began life as a company-funded project in 1954. The Air Force gave approval for the modification of a production F-100C into a two seater. In December 1955 the Air Force authorized production of the two seat version, the **F-100F,** which retained full operational capability. The main differences between it and the single seat versions were in fuel capacity, and in elimination of two of the four M-39 20mm guns in the nose.

The final version of the Super Sabre was the **F-100D,** which was first flown on January 24, 1956. It incorporated flaps, a larger vertical fin, and an autopilot. This was to be the most popular model of the Hun, with 1,274 being produced.

A pair of F-100C-1-NAs get away from Eglin AFB for a practice bomb mission over one of Eglin's ranges during tests of the F-100's newly-designated role of fighter-bomber. May 1956. (USAF)

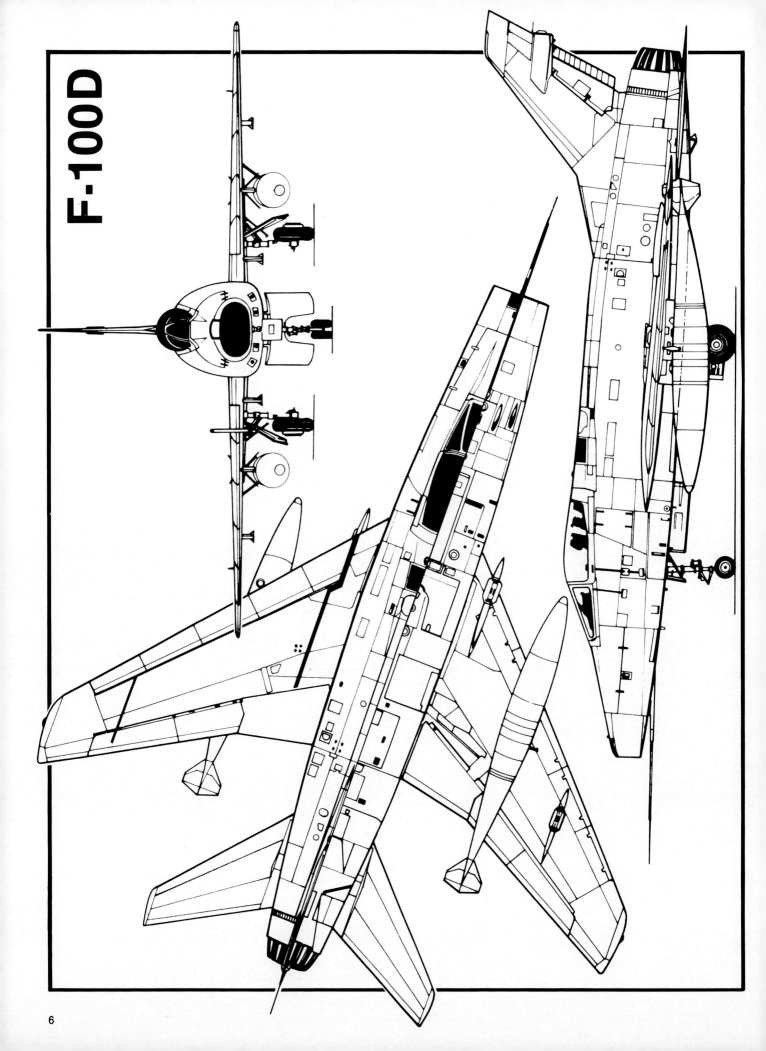

F-100D

F-100C-20-NA of New York Air Guard, 1960. The straight refuelling probe has been replaced by a double bend, bringing the business end up to where it is more visible during hookups with the tanker. (Mort Hartman via Jim Sullivan)

(Right) F-100C-25-NAs at George AFB, California, 1957. (North American)

(Bottom) F-100C of the 479th Fighter Bomber Wing. Wing Commander's aircraft, carries the wing badge on the tail, 435th Fighter Bomber Squadron badge on fuselage. Nose, fuselage, tail bands are, from front to rear, top to bottom: red, yellow, blue, orange, green, edged in white. This looks like the C.O.'s airplane, as it is highly polished! (Dave Menard)

F-100Cs of the 333rd Fighter Bomber Squadron, 4th Fighter Bomber Wing, Seymour-Johnson AFB, late 50s. Markings are red, edged in white. (LtCol George C. Garey via Dave Menard)

F-100C-1-NA fitted with larger fin and heat vent outlet which became standard on the D model, shown on landing rollout at NAA Palmdale facility. (North American)

F-100D-40-NA of the 510th Fighter Bomber Squadron, 405th FBW, Langley AFB, VA, 1957. Wing badge on tail, squadron badge on fuselage. Tail stripe is yellow, edged black. (Menard)

F-1000D-20-NA of USAF Air Research and Development Center, at Edwards AFB Flight Test Center, January, 1958. Besides the modified fin, the D model was the first Hun to be equipped with flaps, wing fences, and, eventually, an arrestor hook. Flaps and the hook were a boon to Hun drivers, since the hot landing A and C models could usually not be stopped without the aid of the drag chute, which had a failure rate in the neighborhood of 5%. (USAF)

F-100D-20-NA of the 531st TFS, 21st TFW, Misawa AFB, Japan in company with RF-101C of 45th TRS, also out of Misawa, refuelling from a KB-50J of the 42ist ARS. Hun markings are red, edged white, while the 101 carries blue and white markings. (Menard)

Ooo-Ha!, an F-100D-25-NA of the 416th TFS, 21st TFW, Misawa AB, 1960. Markings are blue/edged white. (Menard Collection)

Little John, an F-100D-50-NA of the 531st TFS, 39th Air Division, Misawa AB, 1961. All markings are red, edged white with the exception of the drop tank noses, which are dark blue. (Norman E. Taylor via Menard)

F-100Ds of the 531st TFS include Little John and Bonnie Bee (in the foreground). Photographed over Japan, 1961. (USAF)

9

F-100F and D Super Sabres of the 10th TFS, 50th TFW at Toul-Rosieres AB, France, 1959. All markings dark blue with white stars. (Menard)

50th TFW Wing Commander's airplane, 1960-64. Bands on tail are from top; blue, yellow, red with white stars. Worthy of note is the centerline pylon with practice bomb dispenser fitted. Centerline pylon was not often used, since interference with the speed brake was feared. (Menard)

F-100D-90-NA of the 417th TFS, 50th TFW, France, 1959. Markings are red with white stars. 50th TFS Huns carried Squadron badges on tails. (Menard)

(Above) F-100D-25-NA of the 7th TFS, 49th TFW at Toul-Rosieres AB, France 1959, markings are light blue, edged white. (Left) F-100D-90-NA of the 8th TFS, also at Toul-Rosieres in 1959. Markings are yellow, edged black. (Menard)

F-100Ds of the 20th TFW, RAF Wethersfield, United Kingdom, 1961. Fin flashes are (front to rear) red, yellow, blue. Wing badge on tail. (Menard)

F-100D-65-NA of the 79th TFS, 20th TFW, RAF Woodbridge, UK, 1960. This is apparently the Squadron C.O.'s airplane, as it carries stripes on nose. Markings are yellow, edged black. Wing badge on tail, Squadron badge on fuselage with Unit Citation on tail in front of Wing badge. (Menard)

F-100D-65-NA known by the troops as "Triple Zilch" was the Wing C.O.'s steed, with one of many variations on this markings scheme. This one includes blue, yellow, red nose stripes and tail flash, with Squadron badges of 55th, 79th, and 77th TFS on fuselage. (Menard Collection)

F-100D-15-NA of the 48th Fighter Bomber Wing, 1956. Wing C.O.'s airplane had from front; red, yellow, blue fin flash. Wing badge on fuselage under cockpit. Note that this is a polished aluminum aircraft. Whereas, from early '60s on so-called aluminum aircraft were actually painted aluminum. (Menard)

(Left) F-100D-90-NA of the 48th TFW, 492nd TFS at RAF Lakenheath, UK, 1962. Nose and tail chevrons are from front to rear; blue, yellow, red. (G.Pennick via Menard)

F-100Ds of the 35th TFS, 8th TFW, Itazuke AB, Japan, early '60s.

(Above Left) This qualifies as a genuine period piece, illustrating the fighter pilot's love of fast airplanes, cars and....well, something is missing! F-100D of the 36th TFS, 8th TFW, with red, yellow, blue nose chevrons, red tail flashes, all edged in white. Wing badge on fuselage. (Menard)

F-100Fs of 8th TFW, both carrying Wing C.O.'s markings of red, yellow, blue fin flashed refuel from a KB-50J of the 421 ARS over Japan, 1960. (Menard)

F-100D25-NA of the 18th TFW landing at Kadena AFB, Okinawa, 1958. Fin flash from top; red, white, dark blue. Nose flash colors are uncertain, as are colors of wing fences. (USAF via Menard)

F-100D-85-NH gets away from the factory on its delivery flight after undergoing IRAN in early '60s. Flat aluminum finish is most evident in this shot. (North American)

F-100F-10-NA of the 353rd TFS, 354th TFW, 1960. Markings are red and white. (USAF via Menard)

F-100D-85-NH of the 355th TFS, 354th TFW at Aviano, Italy, 1960. Markings are dark green and white. (Menard)

F-100D-90-NA of the 494th, as it appeared in Spring 1959, with red and white markings on spine wingtips and nose. (Dave Menard)

Another F-100D-90-NA of the 494th TFS, 48th TFW at Toul-Rosieres AB, France, Summer 1959. Markings are red and white. Note that the former, much more colorful, nose markings have been overpainted with aluminum. (Dave Menard)

F-100D-70-NA of the 429th Fighter Bomber Squadron, 474th FBW. Markings on nose and tail are yellow and black, while stripes on fuselage and 450 gallon drop tank are, from front to rear: red, yellow, blue, edged black. Arrows on drop tank are yellow and black. (Dave Menard)

(Below Left) F-100D-85-NH of 308th TFS, 31st TFW, with an extremely fresh face on for this 1959 visit to Toul-Rosieres AB. Markings are green and white, with Wing badge on tail. This airplane finished its operational career with the 107th TFS, Michigan Air Guard, and was then transferred to the National Air and Space Museum collection in August 1978. (Menard)

F-100F-15-NA of the 308th TFS, 31st TFW, 1959. (Menard)

F-100D-45-NH of the 511th FBS, 405th FBW, May 1959. Markings are blue and white, with Wing badge on tail. (Merle Olmsted via Menard)

F-100F-10-NA of the 614th FBS, 401st FBW, 1959. Markings on nose are red, black checkerboard over natural aluminum on tail, light grey painted fin cap. 614th badge under cockpit left side, 401st badge same position right side. (Menard)

F-100D-50-NA of the 454th FBS, 323rd FBW, Bunker Hill AFB, Indiana, 1957. Markings are black and white checkerboards with medium blue bands. 454th badge under cockpit. (Balogh via Menard)

1. DROP TANK FUEL QUANTITY GAGE TEST BUTTON
2. DROP TANK FUEL QUANTITY GAGES
3. DRAG CHUTE HANDLE
4. AC LOADMETER
5. DC LOADMETER
6. STATUS DISPLAY LIGHTS
7. ENGINE COMPARTMENT FIRE AND OVERHEAT
8. MASTER HEADING INDICATOR
9. ATTITUDE INDICATOR
10. TRIGGER SAFETY SWITCH
11. ATTITUDE INDICATOR FAST ERECTION BUTTON
12. TACAN-NAVS CHANGE-OVER BUTTON ★
13. NOSE-TAIL RADAR WARNING LIGHTS ★
14. MASTER CAUTION LIGHT
15. HYDRAULIC PRESSURE GAGE SELECTOR SWITCH
16. TURN-AND-SLIP INDICATOR
17. HYDRAULIC PRESSURE GAGE
18. ACCELEROMETER
19. OIL PRESSURE GAGE
20. LABS RELEASE INDICATOR LIGHT
21. TACHOMETER
22. EXHAUST TEMPERATURE GAGE
23. ENGINE PRESSURE RATIO GAGE
24. LANDING GEAR EMERGENCY LOWERING HANDLE
25. LABS DIVE-AND-ROLL INDICATOR
26. FUEL FLOW INDICATOR
27. FUEL QUANTITY GAGE TEST BUTTON
28. FUEL QUANTITY GAGE (TOTAL TANKS)
29. VERTICAL VELOCITY INDICATOR
30. FUEL QUANTITY GAGE (FORWARD TANK)
31. FUEL BOOST PUMP INOP LIGHT
32. COURSE INDICATOR
33. TACAN RANGE INDICATOR
34. LADD RELEASE TIMER
35. RELIEF CONTAINER
36. FOOT-WARMER LEVER
37. TRP TIMER
38. CENTER PEDESTAL
39. IN-FLIGHT CONTROL TESTER PANEL
40. SPECIAL STORE UNLOCKED INDICATOR LIGHT

41. SPECIAL STORE UNLOCK HANDLE
42. RADIO MAGNETIC INDICATOR
43. EXTERNAL LOAD EMERGENCY JETTISON HANDLE
44. SIGHT SELECTOR UNIT
45. ALTIMETER
46. STAND-BY ATTITUDE INDICATOR
47. TACAN INDICATOR LIGHT ★
48. CLOCK
49. GUN SELECTOR SWITCH
50. AIRSPEED/MACH INDICATOR
51. COMMAND RADIO REMOTE CHANNEL INDICATOR

★ Deactivated

Thunderbirds going over the top of a loop in their F-100Cs. Note that they did not have refuelling probes on these aircraft, which limited them to shows within continental U.S. The Skyblazers, also flying F-100Cs, represented the USAFE. When the Thunderbirds got seven league boots, in the form of aerial refuelling capacity, they became the Air Force's official flight demonstration team and the Skyblazers were disbanded. (USAF)

F-100D-30-NA of the 1964 Thunderbirds team. Aircraft serials were carried until late 1965, when they were replaced with individual formation numbers spelled out. (Paul Stevens)

F-100D of Thunderbird's leader, Major Neil Eddins, as it appeared for 1967 show at Chanute AFB, Ill. (Paul Stevens)

F-100D solo aircraft during low pass at Wilmington, N.C. in 1968, the last year in which the Thunderbirds flew the Hun. (Jim Sullivan)

Thunderbird #5 making a go-around at Wilmington, N.C. April 21, 1968, with just about everything hanging out except the drag chute. (Jim Sullivan)

Drag Chute deployment sequence is illustrated here, as pilot chute has pulled deployment bag containing drag chute from its compartment under aft fuselage, cable has released from spring steel panels on aft fuselage side, and is about to pull taut. (Jim Sullivan)

F-100D positioned on ZEL (zero length launch) platform at Nellis AFB, Nevada. Rocketdyne M-34 solid rocket motor developing 130,000 lbs. of thrust is mounted under aft fuselage. It will provide a 4G push through 275 knots, at which time the pilot will jettison the rocket engine and continue the mission. First launch occured in March 1958. All of the final blocks of D and F Huns were ZEL-capable, though only 20 additional launches were made.

F-100s were among the first combat aircraft committed to the Vietnam War, seen here at Bien Hoa AB in the early '60s. (USAF)

F-100D-85-NH of the 617th TFS, 37th TFW in the arming pits at Phan Rang AB, RVN, prior to May 1969 mission. Armorers will remove all safety pins from ordnance before waving the Huns out for takeoff. Arming pit is usually close to the end of the active runway, well away from the parking ramp. (USAF)

F-100D-70-NA of the 531st TFS, 3rd TFW taxis in post mission, Bien Hoa AB, RVN, December 1969. Fin tip and crew name block are red, with white trim. (USAF)

F-100C-1-NA of the 121st TFS, District of Columbia Air Guard, at Andrews AFB, MD, 1967.

(Above Right) France received 75 F-100Ds and 7 F-100Fs under the MAP. These were operated by 11 Escadre De Chasse (illustrated) and 3 Escadre De Chasse. French Huns may well have been the first of the type to see combat, flying missions to Algeria in 1960. (Michel C. Klaver)

F-100D-40-NH of 730 Squadron, Royal Danish Air Force, 1962. Nose and tail markings are blue and white. Denmark received 50 Ds and 8 Fs under MAP. They were operated by 725, 727, and 730 Eskadrillerne. (via Paul Stevens)

F-100 Aircraft Marking Specification

	MARKING	LOCATION	SIZE	FS COLOR NO.
A	U.S. AIR FORCE	Both sides of fuselage	Letters 15" high	15044
B	Model Designation, Acft S/N and fuel requirement	Left side of fuselage	Letters and numbers 1" high	17038
C	National Star	Both sides of fuselage	25" star	Background border-15044, Stars and Bars-17875, Stripes-11136
D		On under surface of right wing and top surface of left wing	35" star	
E	USAF	Top surface of right wing and under surface of left wing	30" high letters	15044
F	Call Numbers	Both sides of vertical stabilizer	12" high numbers	17038
G	Arctic Markings	One inch clearance around all large insignia and lettering		12197
H	Anti-Glare	Top of fuselage in front of cockpit		37038

Standard USAF Camouflage

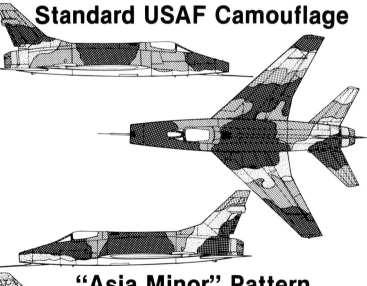

"Asia Minor" Pattern

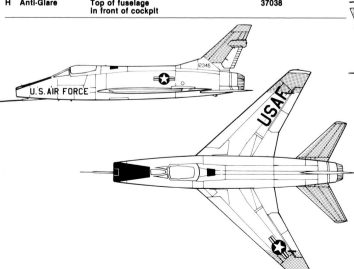

The third F-101A lands at Lambert Field, St. Louis, after its maiden flight on November 26, 1954. McDonnell's chief test pilot, Bob Little, was at the controls. (USAF)

McDonnell F-101 Voodoo

Whoever said that truth was stranger than fiction was certainly blessed with some extreme insight. Take, for instance, the case of McDonnell's first supersonic fighter, The One-O-Wonder-ful Voodoo. Its early history was a succession of fits and starts, as the USAF attempted to put some perspective to the technological innovations that were pouring forth from the aircraft designers of America.

The 101 was sired by the XF-88, which grew from the post World War II need for a long-range fighter to escort SAC's bombers. SAC was everything in those days. If they said they needed fighters, well, then they were going to get them! The first XF-88 took to the air in October 1948, powered by a pair of 3,000 lb. thrust J-34s. The second XF-88 was cancelled in August 1950.

What SAC thought it could do without in 1950, it found out it couldn't live without in 1951. MiG-15s were making life miserable for B-29 crews attempting daylight missions over the Yalu. Suddenly, the XF-88 was on again. McDonnell was aware that the marginal performance of the XF-88, with its J-34 engines, would kill the program as soon as the panic of Korean War experiences began to fade. The J-57 engine was now available. Project Engineer Edward M. Flesh proposed that the XF-88 be stretched to accomodate the bigger and more powerful engine. The Air Force couldn't have been happier with this proposal, a contract being issued in January 1952 for 31 pre-production **F-101As.**

The first F-101A made its maiden flight on September 29, 1954 at Edwards Air Force Base. The Air Force planned on equipping five wings with the Voodoo, and it looked as if McDonnell had hit the aerospace jackpot. Unfortunately, flight testing revealed some serious problems. The basic problem had to do with the stabilator, which, being mounted high on the vertical fin, was prone to being blanketed out at high angle of attack. The Air Force ordered suspension of further production of the F-101 on May 23, 1956. Following the suspension of production, questions again arose concerning the basic F-101 mission.

The first flight of the Voodoo had seen a dramatic shift in mission emphasis. As SAC dropped its option on that day, TAC picked it up, deciding that the erstwhile escort fighter would now become a penetration fighter-bomber. By 1956, TAC had assigned the fighter bomber role to the F-100, which seemed to have taken to the role ad-

mirably. Still, both the Air Force and McDonnell had a lot of time and money invested in the 101 program. Neither of them really wanted to see it all go down the tubes. A large effort by both service and contractor engineers finally resolved the technical problems and McDonnell was allowed to resume production in November 1956. Initial configuration of the Voodoo included four M-39 20mm cannon, two retractable rocket pods each carrying six 2.75 inch rockets and three AIM-4A Falcon radar-homing AAMs which were mounted on a rotary weapons bay door in the fuselage. It carried APS-54 radar, had a total fuel capacity which gave it an unrefuelled range of 1,700 miles at 0.9 mach at 36,000 feet and was generally just what SAC had wanted in its escort fighter.

The first of 50 production F-101As was delivered to the 81st TFW in May 1957. TAC had insisted upon changes to the basic configuration, making it more suitable to the tactical fighter role. These included deletion of one of the starboard M-39s to make room for TACAN, deletion of retractable rocket pods and addition of a centerline stores hardpoint to allow the 101 to carry a nuclear bomb. The escort fighter had become the bomber! Structural beef-up to the airframe to allow low-level high speed penetrations, begun with the 51st production airplane, resulted in redesignation to **F-101C.** A total of 124 F-101A and C models were built, including the 29 pre-production airplanes which, incidentally, remained in flight test units.

The single seat Voodoo earned its niche in the aviation hall of fame in the reconnaissance role. TAC hedged its bets on the 101 in 1954, ordering two recce examples, designated **YRF-101A.** The first of these flew in May 1956. The RF version of the basic 101 design featured a longer nose, which carried from four to six high speed framing cameras. The first wing to operate the RF-101 was the 63rd TRW, which received the first of its airplanes in May 1957. A total of 35 **RF-101As** were built before the previously mentioned airframe strengthening program resulted in a switch to **RF-101C** production. The first RF-101C flew in July 1957. A total of 166 Cs were built. Communist Chinese threats of direct action against Formosa resulted in a show of force in support of the Nationalist Government in 1957. Six RF-101As of the 17th TRS flew from Shaw AFB, S.C. to Formosa, using in-flight refuelling and rest stops at island bases across the Pacific. This set the stage for trans-Pacific delivery flights of the RF-101C to the 45th TRS at Misawa AB, Japan and the 15th TRS at Kadena AB, Okinawa in 1958.

The first 101 combat missions were very likely flown by Voodoos in the markings of Nationalist China, which received from 6 to 9 of the RFs in 1959. With the RF-101, the Nationalists were able to photograph strips of the mainland up to 100 miles inland, without actually violating communist airspace. Naturally, they weren't satisfied with this. They had a recce fighter hotter than anything their enemies on the mainland could put up. They used the 101's altitude and speed advantage to photograph anything and everything within range. Eventually the communists got hotter airplanes and surface to air missiles. Operational attrition of one kind or another is thought to have finally eliminated the 101 from the Nationalist Chinese Air Force.

RF-101s performed invaluable service in the Cuban missile crisis of 1962 and went on to distinguish themselves in Vietnam. The first 101s to arrive in Southeast Asia visited Don Muang and Tao Yuan in Thailand in 1960. This was followed by a visit of four RF-101s to Tan Son Nhut in 1961, during General Maxwell D. Taylor's fact-finding mission for JFK. The RFs remained after Taylor had gone, ostensibly to log some flying time, but actually to keep an eye on communist activity and to report on any Viet Cong or North Vietnamese build-up. From these seemingly insignificant beginnings, the American involvement in the region continued to expand. The RF-101 was never out of Southeast Asia until finally being withdrawn from operational use, in favor of the RF-4C, in 1968.

The final, and most numerous, model of the basic 101 design was the **F-101B.** The B made its first flight on March 27, 1957. It had been ordered as a result of problems with the fledgling F-102. (Such was the cornucopia of technology flowing from the fertile drawing boards of American aircraft companies, that the Air Force, if not satisfied with the progress of one of its programs, could simply adapt another program to fit the mission.)

The F-101B was destined to become the longest-lived of the series, as it continues to soldier on into the 'eighties. Changes from the basic design include addition of a second seat for the radar observer, the MG-13 fire control system, provision for three Falcon AAMs in a rotary weapons bay door and external hardpoints to accomodate a pair of AIR-2A Genie AAMs with nuclear warheads. The first F-101B to enter ADC inventory was delivered in January 1959. By August 1960, 17 ADC Squadrons had received the F-101B. It replaced the F-86L, F-89J, F-102, and F-104 in these squadrons and would remain a principle ingredient in America's deterrent to enemy air attack for over two decades. A total of 478 Bs were built. In 1961, 66 of them were transferred to the RCAF, after modifictions made to suit Canadian requirements. The modified F-101Bs were redesignated Fs.

F-101B under test at Edwards with two nuclear armed MB-1 Genie AAMs on fuselage pallet. (USAF)

Pre-production F-101A at Edwards AFB, June 1956, with flaps down and speed brakes out. Note control positions with full right rudder and aileron. (USAF)

All 29 pre-production F-101As were retained in test status after production airplanes went into the inventory. This aircraft is shown at Edwards in 1958, wearing the badge of the flight test center on the tail. (USAF)

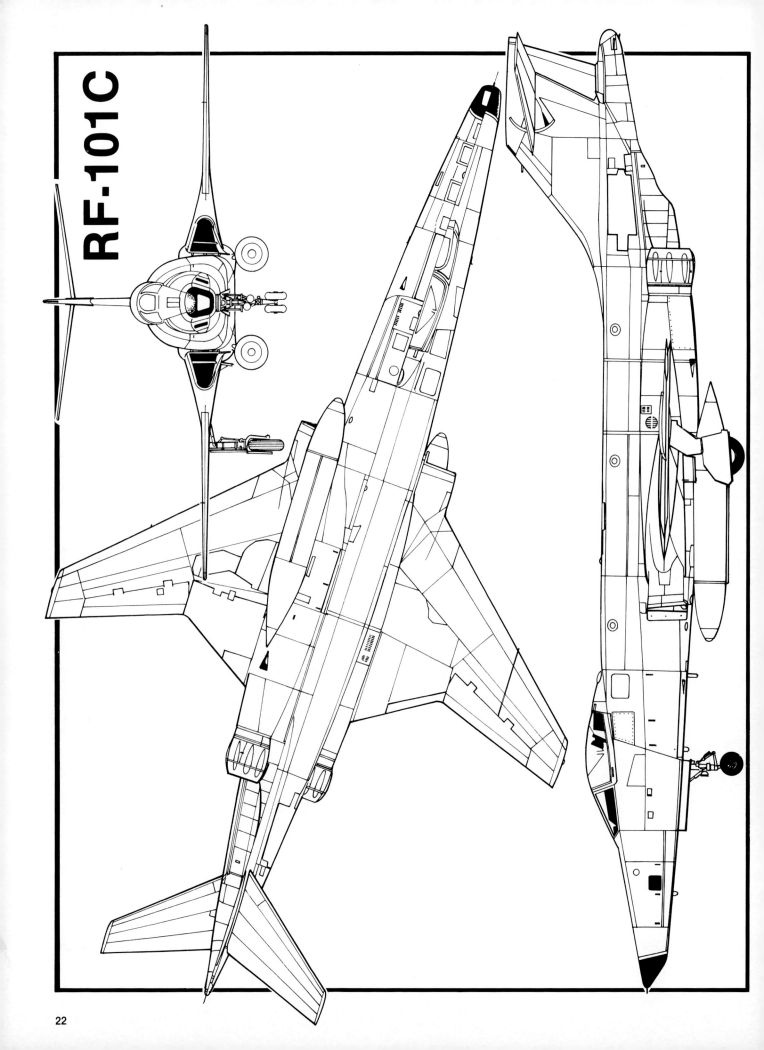

RF-101C

1/Lt. Jules F. Nielsen, Jr. of Elmhurst, Ill. strikes a pose in front of the 101 he flew from Andrews AFB to Lieze, Belgium with the aid of refuelling from KC-135 tanker. F-101A carries the markings of the 522nd FBS, 27th FBW. It was based at Bergstrom AFB, Texas. (USAF)

Two detail shots of the F-101A flown by Major John Burns, of the 81st TFW (also see color rendering).

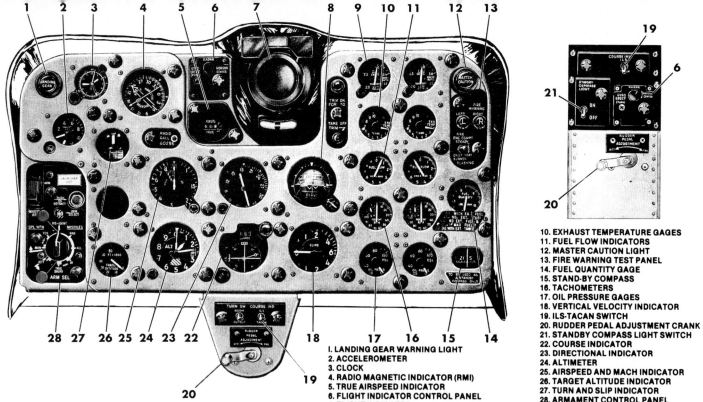

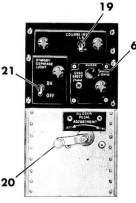

10. EXHAUST TEMPERATURE GAGES
11. FUEL FLOW INDICATORS
12. MASTER CAUTION LIGHT
13. FIRE WARNING TEST PANEL
14. FUEL QUANTITY GAGE
15. STAND-BY COMPASS
16. TACHOMETERS
17. OIL PRESSURE GAGES
18. VERTICAL VELOCITY INDICATOR
19. ILS-TACAN SWITCH
20. RUDDER PEDAL ADJUSTMENT CRANK
21. STANDBY COMPASS LIGHT SWITCH
22. COURSE INDICATOR
23. DIRECTIONAL INDICATOR
24. ALTIMETER
25. AIRSPEED AND MACH INDICATOR
26. TARGET ALTITUDE INDICATOR
27. TURN AND SLIP INDICATOR
28. ARMAMENT CONTROL PANEL

1. LANDING GEAR WARNING LIGHT
2. ACCELEROMETER
3. CLOCK
4. RADIO MAGNETIC INDICATOR (RMI)
5. TRUE AIRSPEED INDICATOR
6. FLIGHT INDICATOR CONTROL PANEL
7. FLIGHT INDICATOR
8. ATTITUDE INDICATOR
9. ENGINE PRESSURE RATIO GAGES

Pristine F-101A prior to its delivery flight. The F-101A captured the world's absolute speed record on December 12, 1957, posting a two-way average speed of 1207.6 mph over a ten mile course. The record flight was flown by Major Adrian E. Drew of the 27th FBW at 39,000 feet over Edwards AFB, California. (Paul Stevens)

F-101C of the 81st TFW. This aircraft was later converted to RF-101H. Markings on tail are top to bottom; medium blue, yellow, red, with white or blue stars. Wing badge on both sides of fuselage. (Paul Stevens)

RF-101C of the 363rd TRW, 17th TRS, at Andrews AFB, October 1957. (USAF)

(Above Right) RF-101C of the 17th TRS as it appeared during the November 1957 mobilization exercise MOBILE ZEBRA, which saw units of TAC's Ninth and Eighteenth Air Forces fly to the far east. (USAF)

RF-101C of the 17th TRS. Checkerboard on tail is light red, similar to FS 21158. Band on nose is apparently a darker red. Note that badge has been removed from nose. (via Paul Stevens)

RF-101Cs of the Nationalist Chinese Air Force, photographed in 1966. Supplied with between 6 and 9 RF-101s in 1959, the Chinese Nationalists operated them successfully over the mainland for several years before operational attrition finally ended their careers. (Sullivan)

RF-101C of the 363rd TRW. This aircraft has red nose band, whereas our cover airplane carried a dark blue band. (USAF)

RF-101C's nose opened up to expose its cameras. KA-2s and KA-45s were carried prior to 1964 modernization, which included replacement of these cameras with the Hycon KS-72A cameras. (Roger Besecker)

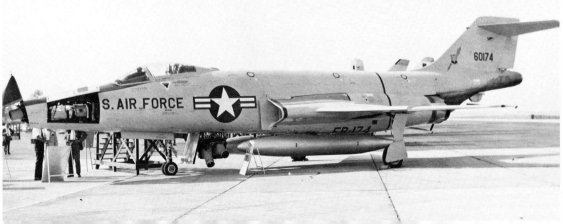

25

Official markings scheme carried from 1960 until the introduction of camouflage in the mid-sixties was overall gloss grey, with TAC badge and lightning bolt on tail, illustrated by this RF-101 at Eglin AFB, Florida, 4487th Test Squadron, September 1964. (Norman E Taylor via Paul Stevens)

First attempts at camouflaging the RF-101 (and perhaps the first attempt at camouflaging any TAC aircraft!) was during the Cuban missile crisis of 1962. Colors are two shades of green, and entire aircraft has been painted, including nose and exhausts! (USAF via Paul Stevens)

Another early camouflage scheme is modelled by the RF-101C during Strike Command's exercise GOLDFIRE, which was held in the area of Ft. Leonard Wood, MO in November 1964. Colors are two shades of green, one shade of brown. Light colored band on fuselage was a marking applied for this exercise only. (USAF)

First RF-101s to deploy to Vietnam wore the TAC grey scheme. This one has the PACAF badge on its tail, Tan Son Nhut AB, RVN, February 1964. (USAF)

(Below Right) RF-101A-25-MC of the 4414th CCTS, Shaw AFB, S.C., March 1966. Camouflage scheme is olive drab, dark green, and medium brown, with the brown being the lightest appearing color in this photo. (Norman E. Taylor)

The same aircraft on final approach at Shaw AFB, September 1966. (Jim Sullivan)

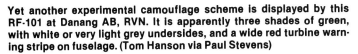

Yet another experimental camouflage scheme is displayed by this RF-101 at Danang AB, RVN. It is apparently three shades of green, with white or very light grey undersides, and a wide red turbine warning stripe on fuselage. (Tom Hanson via Paul Stevens)

Camouflage colors, if not patterns, had been standardized by 1968. This well-worn veteran was a part of the big recce effort expended during Rolling Thunder, Tan Son Nhut AB, 1968. (USAF)

Major James F. Young of the 20th TRS taxies in after a mission over North Vietnam in 1966. (USAF)

Late model RF-101 nose, showing pitot and sensor heads, as well as camera windows. (USAF)

Slightly non-standard camouflage treatment, as evidenced by large national insignia on fuselage, service name on fuselage and treatment of aircraft serial number was still carried by some RF-101s of the 363rd TRW at Shaw AFB in 1966. (Jim Sullivan)

Standard camouflage pattern on an RF-101 of the 18th TRS, landing at Shaw, 1970. (Jim Sullivan)

(Left and Below) Two variations on camouflage pattern as applied to subsequently numbered airplanes. The recce Voodoo performed yeoman service in Southeast Asia, performing the majority of pre- and post-strike work during Rolling Thunder. The Voodoo was successful in spite of a nasty predeliction to pitch up when excessive angles of attack were put on it, as might be expected to occur when a pilot was attempting to evade a SAM or AAA. (Paul Stevens)

(Above and Right) Two views of the prototype RF-101F, as it appeared at Greenville, S.C. in August 1971. It had been dubbed "2,000 MPH Brownie Camera"...obviously by someone who was not familiar with its performance figures. (Jim Sullivan)

79 of the 480 B models built were modified with dual controls for transition training. These were redesignated F-101F. Some of these did not have the intercept radar gear and were later modified into RF-101Fs. This aircraft belonged to the 192nd TRS of the Nevada Air Guard in 1972. (Jerry Geer via Paul Stevens)

F-101B leads a formation of the ADC allstars. (USAF)

Freshly minted F-101B awaits delivery to its operational home from the McDonnell factory. The 101 remained true to its original mission(s) throughout its service life, one of the few modern aircraft that were not modified for something other than the designer's original intent. (Paul Stevens)

(Below Left) F-101B-105-MC landing at Greenville, S.C. in May 1971. The F-101B was operated by up to 26 Squadrons during its USAF career. (Jim Sullivan)

F-101B-95-MC of the 60th FIS, Otis AFB, Mass. May 1960. The 60th was the first unit to get the F-101B. Tail markings are red, while the B on the intake ramp is black. (Thomas S. Cuddy II via Paul Stevens)

Relatively large flap area is displayed in this head-on shot on an F-101B. (S. Ohtaki)

F-101B-110-MC of the 29th FIS, with afterburners ablaze, takes off from Malmstrom AFB, Montana in 1966. Tail flash is yellow, with black edges. ADC badge on starboard side of tail, Squadron badge on left side. (USAF)

Latest markings of F-101B of the 107th TFG are also the last to be displayed on a Voodoo by this unit. They include Squadron badge, ANG shield, and ADC pennant on tail. (S. Ohtaki)

F-101B of the 123rd FIS, 142nd FG, Oregon ANG at William Tell '78. Red bird, with yellow beak, trimmed in black. Black scroll with white lettering. Insides of all gear doors, speed brakes, flaps are gloss red. (S. Ohtaki)

Mothballs! The eventual fate of all F-101s is displayed by this Voodoo of the Washington ANG, at Greenville, S. C. in 1971. (Jim Sullivan)

During 1961, the RCAF acquired 56 F-101Bs and 10 F-101Fs (the F is the dual control model) to replace its CF-100 interceptors. These were taken directly from operational ADC squadrons, the Canadians eliminating the fiscal year prefix from the serial number, and adding a 17. Note that some vestiges of the USAF markings remain on these aircraft. (RCAF via Paul Stevens)

As the F-101 was phased out of active ADC service, 66 of them were extensively modernized and turned over to the Canadian Armed Forces, in exchange for the 58 remaining original CF-101s. These were assigned completely new serial numbers by Canada, beginning with 101001. These CF-101s belong to 409 Squadron, flying out of Comox, B.C. This is the current CAF markings scheme. (via Paul Stevens)

CF-101 fires a Genie. This Voodoo belongs to 425 Squadron "Alouettes", out of Bagotville. CAF aircraft were bilingual at this time, with French on the right side and English on the left. (via Paul Stevens)

F-100 Super Sabre

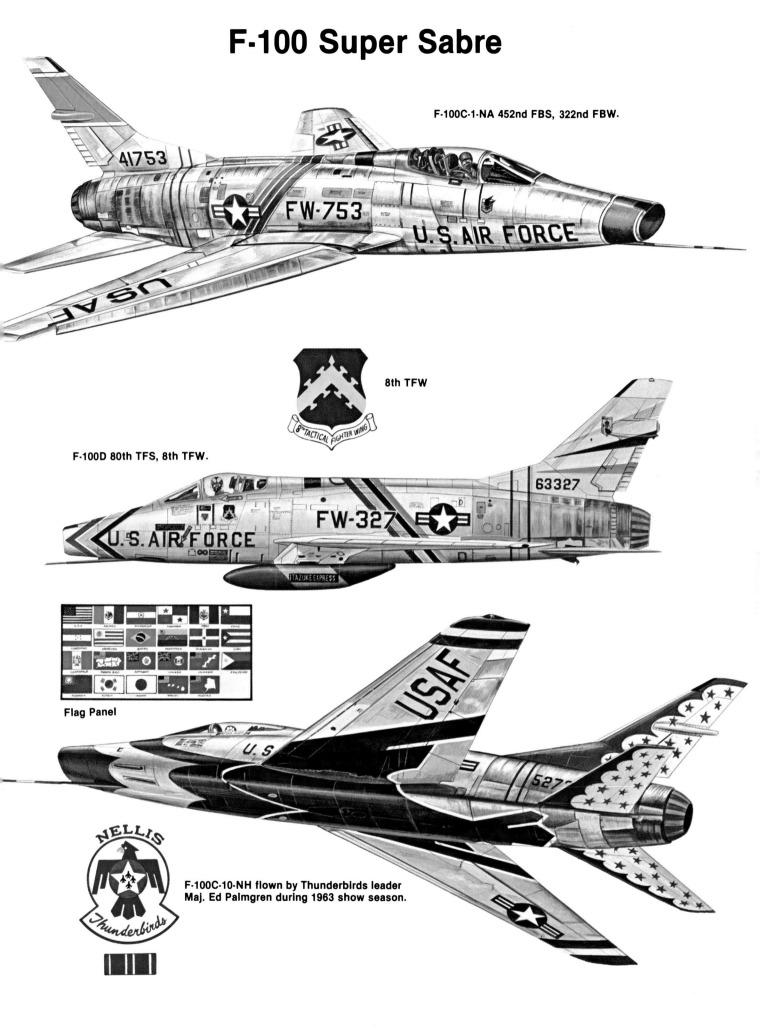

F-100C-1-NA 452nd FBS, 322nd FBW.

8th TFW

8TH TACTICAL FIGHTER WING

F-100D 80th TFS, 8th TFW.

Flag Panel

NELLIS
Thunderbirds

F-100C-10-NH flown by Thunderbirds leader
Maj. Ed Palmgren during 1963 show season.

CF-101B of 409 Squadron at William Tell '78. The Canadian Squadrons are an integral part of NORAD and participate in all competitions. CF-101s are now painted overall gloss grey. (S. Ohtaki)

CF-101B of 416 Squadron, as it appeared during 1971 visit to Greenville, S.C. It was home-based at CAF Chatham. Though this aircraft is natural metal, most Canadian 101s were painted aluminum soon after this photo was taken. (Jim Sullivan)

CF-101Bs of 425 Squadron, illustrate the painted aluminum look. Squadron badge is red and black, white lettering. (Paul Stevens)

F/RF-101 Aircraft Marking Specification

MARKING	LOCATION	SIZE	FS COLOR NO
A U.S. AIR FORCE	Both sides of fuselage	Letters 12" high	15044
B Model Designation, Acft S/N and fuel Requirement	Left side of fuselage	Letters and numbers 1" high	17038
C National Star	Both sides of fuselage	40" star	Background, border - 15044, Stars and Bars - 17875, Stripes - 11136
D	On under surface of right wing and top surface of left wing	35" star	
E USAF	On under surface of left wing and upper surface of right wing	Letters 25" high	15044
F Call Numbers	Both sides of vertical stabilizer	12" high numbers	17038
G Arctic Markings	One inch clearance around all large insignia and lettering		12197
H Anti-Glare	Top of fuselage in front of cockpit		37038

Standard USAF Camouflage

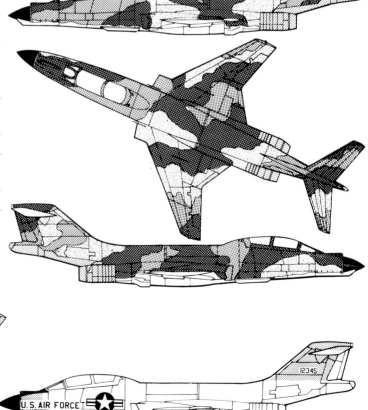

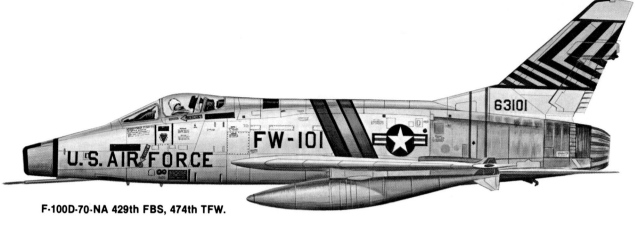

F-100D-70-NA 429th FBS, 474th TFW.

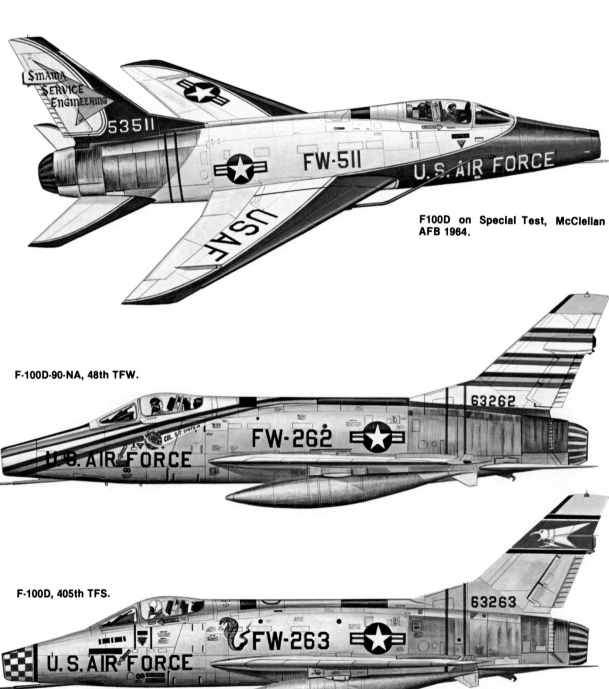

F100D on Special Test, McClellan AFB 1964.

F-100D-90-NA, 48th TFW.

F-100D, 405th TFS.

F-100D of French AF, June 1978.

F-100F-10-NA of the 353rd TFS, 354th TFW.

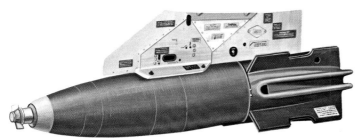

Mk 81 Snakeye I 250 lb. GP Bomb

F-100 Ejection Seat

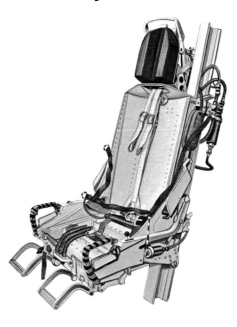

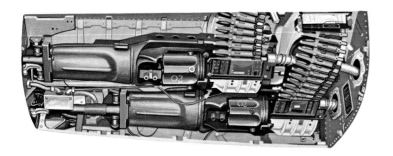

F-100 port gun bay showing two of the four M-39 Automatic Guns. These 20mm weapons are Gas-Operated, Belt-Fed and Electrically Fired revolver-type guns.

F-102 Delta Dagger

The F-102 was the first weapons system to be designed from the drawing board up. "Weapons system" is a term we have come to take for granted, but in 1950 it had not yet entered the lexicon of aerospace terminology. The very idea of such a thing was somewhat revolutionary. The fact that the weapons system would be wrapped up in a delta-winged package made it seem down-right Buck Rogers!

The F-102 story really starts in 1945, when teams from American aircraft companies were scouring a ravaged Germany for talent and ideas. (We had the industrial wherewithal to bury the Axis in World War II, but the Germans really had cornered the market on innovative aerospace ideas.) One of the more interesting concepts to make it to this side of the Atlantic was the delta-winged fighter of Dr. Alex Lippisch, who had designed the Me 163 Komet. The intra-service rivalry of our Army and Navy had survived the war in robust good health, being manifested by both services awarding contracts for delta-winged fighters. Teams from Convair and Douglas were in on the ground floor and they received the contracts. The Air Force contract to Convair was for a Mach 1.2 fighter. This in 1945, before anyone had even flown faster than the speed of sound! The contract was amended the following year to provide for one research aircraft only, the eventual result being the **XF-92A**, which flew for the first time on June 9, 1948. The XF-92A was far from supersonic, but it was extremely successful in proving the concept of a delta-winged fighter. All it needed, they thought, was a bigger engine....then it would be supersonic. They were in for a rude awakening.

By 1949 the Air Force had reached some conclusions about air defense tactics and equipment that required some fundamental changes in the way interceptors were designed. In the first place, since the enemy bombers would be carrying nuclear bombs, you had to try to bring everyone of them down. In order to do that, you would have to have a lot of interceptors or you would have to arm the interceptors that you had with very effective weapons that could be fired from greater distances than the conventional air-to-air weapons (guns) of the day. There had been some moderately successful use of airborne radar in the war and improvments were being made all the time. This, coupled with unguided aerial rockets, provided the basis for the first primitive weapons systems which were embodied in F-94 and F-89 aircraft

Hughes Aircraft Company had pioneered the field of Airborne Intercept Radar. It was their E-4 radar that equipped the F-89 and F-86D. They received the contract for the MX-1179 system, which would detect and track a target and guide weapons to it from the intercep-

tor. The interceptor had yet to be designed, but the Air Force did send out Request For Proposals in 1950 and they did invite Convair to bid on the project. Convair's bid was based upon its very successful XF-92A. They were awarded a contract for two prototypes in December 1951. The problems involved in this ambitious project were really quite staggering at the time. First of all, a supersonic fighter was going to have to be designed. The contractor was proposing a radical configuration. Secondly, a radar and fire-control system was going to have to be designed and built parallel to the fighter design. The two systems then had to merge at the end of their gestation period and work well together. This was the birth of the modern weapons system. A third complication was added to this scenario. In the early 'fifties it looked as though we really needed an interceptor fast. The sooner, the better! The designers really could not afford to waste any time in getting the system from concept to reality. The Air Force indicated that they wanted the interceptor in the inventory by 1954.

Because the whole system had become so complicated, it became obvious that a pure 'experimental' version of the final product could not be handbuilt, tested, reworked, tested again, etc., etc. There just wasn't the time for that. The designers would have to give it their best shot and come up with the production article the first time around. This philosophy was articulated by Air Force Generals Orval R. Cook and Lawrence Craigie and the die was cast. The Cook-Craigie Plan became the standard for Air Force weapons system procurement. This really puts the onus on the designer to come up with the best compromise between practicality and advanced features. In retrospect, it appears to have been a stroke of genius, as it has allowed the United States to develope and build the most advanced weapons systems in the world

The prototype F-102 was designated **YF-102.** It was about 25% larger than its progenitor, the XF-92A, and powered by the wonder engine of the '50s, the J-57. It made its first flight on October 24, 1953 at Edwards AFB, with Convair's Chief Project Test Pilot Richard L. Johnson at the controls. Testing continued with Johnson, Earle G. Martin and Sam Shannon sharing the duty. As they approached the Mach, they encountered all kinds of problems, including severe buffet and yaw oscillation. To cap it off, on its seventh flight the YF-102 suffered a flame-out and crash-landing which destroyed number one prototype. The second prototype was rolled out and flown on January 11, 1954, but despite the modifications made to damp out the buffet and yaw, it just would not break Mach 1. The vehicle that would carry the ultra-sophisticated MX-1179 system into battle wouldn't even break the Mach! Things looked very dark indeed for the F-102, and it was at this point that the Air Force got McDonnell cracking on the F-101B.

What had led Convair to this dismal day? Well, to put it into a neat little package, I would have to say that the absence of a supersonic wind tunnel had done them in. On paper the YF-102 was supersonic, but the principle for design of supersonic wind tunnels was not elucidated until 1949 by NACA's John Stack. The first supersonic wind tunnel became operational in 1951 at Langley Laboratory. Unfortunately, by that time all the design work had been done on the 102 and it was in the works. Experimentation at Langley led to the "Area Rule" of aerodynamics, authored by Richard T. Whitcomb. This led to the so-called "coke bottle" fuselage. When the F-102 got into serious trouble, Convair decided to make use of area rule theory, which had been made public in December 1953.

Convair produced the **YF-102A** in 117 days of around-the-clock labor at their San Diego plant. It only barely resembled the original YF-102. The fuselage was 16 feet longer, had that coke bottle shape, along with a drooped nose and a new canopy. It had an uprated engine, the J-57-P41, which gave 15,500 lb. of thrust. The YF-102A made its first flight on December 20,1954, going through the Mach, to 1.2, the following day. The following month it climbed to over 55,000 feet and the Air Force, and Convair, breathed a collective sigh of relief.

Even though they now felt they had the production configuration basically correct and that production could go ahead, their problems were not over. As the flight test program began to explore the region beyond Mach 1.2, severe structural vibration was encountered. It took until January 1956 to work out that problem, the solution of which was a redesigned and strengthened air inlet ramp. Testing continued while airplanes continued to roll off the production line. Everytime a modification became standard as a result of tests, it had to be retrofitted to production airplanes. The classic case in point is the vertical fin, which had been enlarged to give better directional stability. This modification became standard on the 66th airplane and was retrofitted to all previous airplanes. The final production configuration was agreed upon in April 1957 after half of the production batch of 873 102s had been manufactured. Production was completed one year later.

The weapons employed in the production airplane included 3 AIM-4A radar-guided and 3 AIM-4C infra-red homing AAMs. These were carried internally, in the weapons bay in the belly. The folding weapons bay doors originally had provision for accomodation of 24 unguided folding fin aerial rockets. These were eliminated. The initial production version of the MX-1179 weapons system was the MG-3.

The first unit to receive the F-102 was the 327th FIS, which began receiving its aircraft in June 1956. Peak usage of the Deuce came a scant four years later, with 25 ADC squadrons flying the 102. During its service life, the 102 was flown by 46 USAF squadrons, 20 ANG squadrons and by Greece and Turkey. The Air Force has modified several as **QF-102s** and **PQM-102As** for use as drones. Its first line service life was relatively short, only because it had so effectively demonstrated the potential of its basic design, which led to development of the F-106 Delta Dart.

The early windscreen configuration is evident in this shot of the first YF-102. Also note the non-area-ruled fuselage. (USAF)

First flight of the prototype Deuce was made at Edwards AFB, October 1953 by Convair's Richard Johnson. (USAF)

F-101 Voodoo

F-101A of 81st TFW.

F-101 Ejection Seat

F-101 Main Landing Gear

Nose Gear

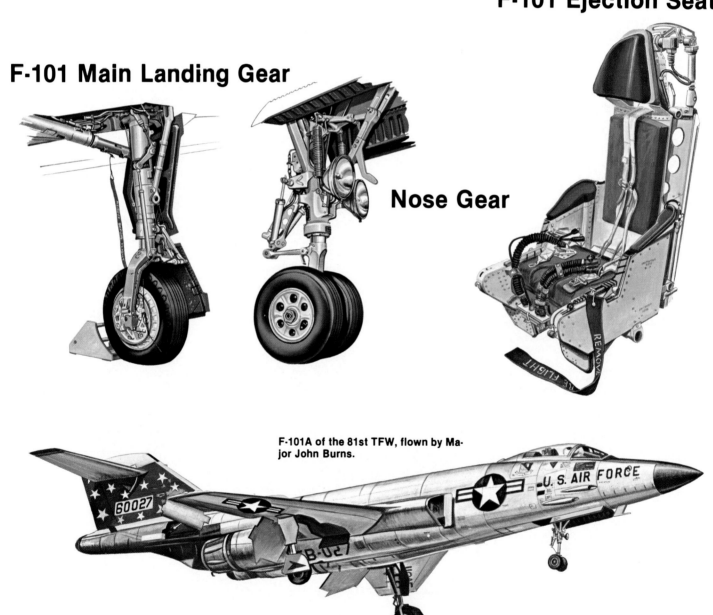

F-101A of the 81st TFW, flown by Major John Burns.

RF-101C of "Operation Sun Run". "Sun Run 3" was flown by Lt. Gus Klatt at an average speed of 781.74 MPH from Los Angeles to New York on November 27, 1957.

F-101B-95-MC of the 60th FIS, L. G. Hanscom Fld., Mass, 1965.

60th FIS

Early RF-101C camouflage trial pattern, as seen at Nellis AFB, Nevada, 1967.

F-101B 105-MC of 132nd FIS, Maine Air Guard, 1974.

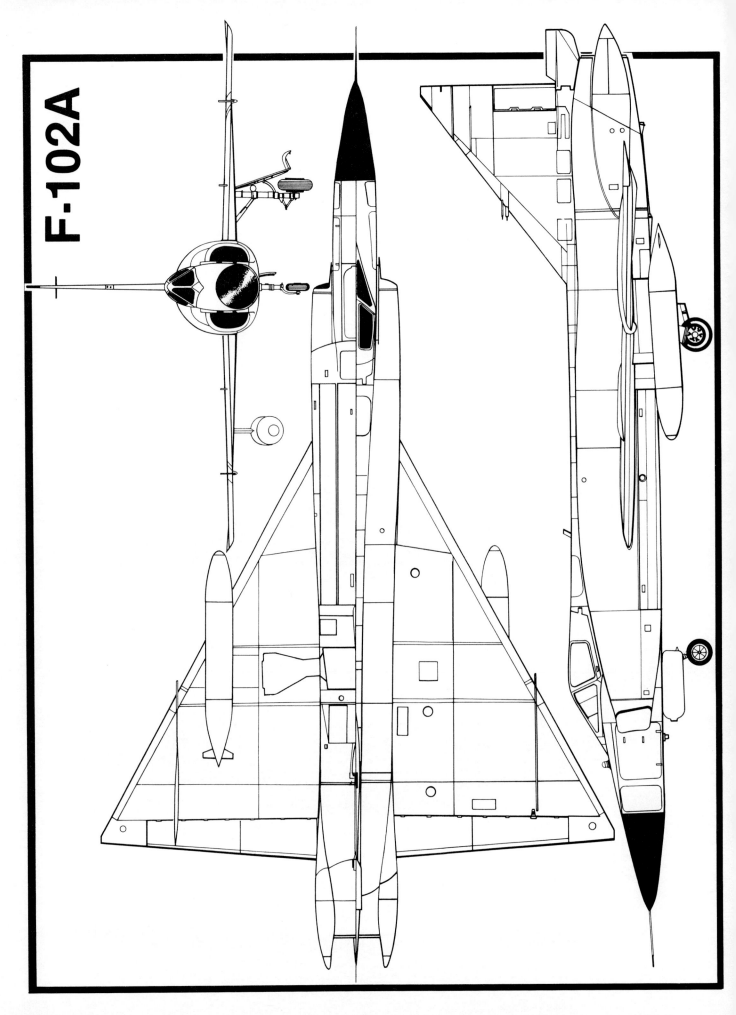

F-102A

The YF-102 consistently refused to fly beyond Mach 1 in level flight, despite the best efforts of Convair's engineers who removed and reworked the wing tips twice and later added an elongated nose. (USAF)

The number two YF-102 took over the bulk of the test program after number one crashed. Power unit for rudder is in fairing on vertical fin, while the elevon units are in the fairings under the wings. (USAF)

The first YF-102A showed a marked difference from the unsuccessful YF-102, with its area-ruled, longer fuselage and 'V' windscreen. (Convair)

First production F-102As had the short vertical fin and were later retrofitted with the larger fin. The 'V' windscreen was adopted to cut drag. It caused so many distracting reflections in the cockpit that a vision splitter was installed. (Peter Bowers via Jim Sullivan)

F-101B of the 142nd FIG Oregon ANG, as it appeared at William Tell '78.

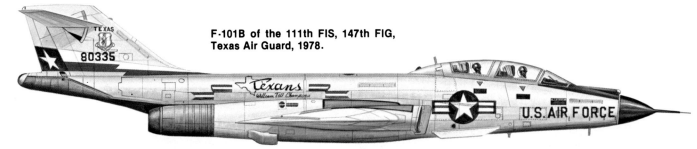

F-101B of the 111th FIS, 147th FIG, Texas Air Guard, 1978.

Auxilliary Power Unit

MJ-1 Bomb Loader with M117 760 lb. GP Bomb

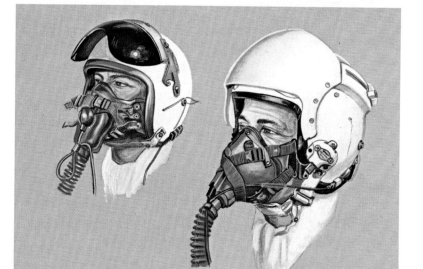

Two types of helmet and oxygen mask worn by Century Series crew. The P-4A helmet and mask (left) was in use during the fifties. The helmet currently in use is individually form-fitted to each pilot and includes clear and tinted visors in its shield. It is used in conjunction with the MBU-5/P mask. (right)

CF-101B of 409 Squadron, CAF, 1977.

F-102 Delta Dagger

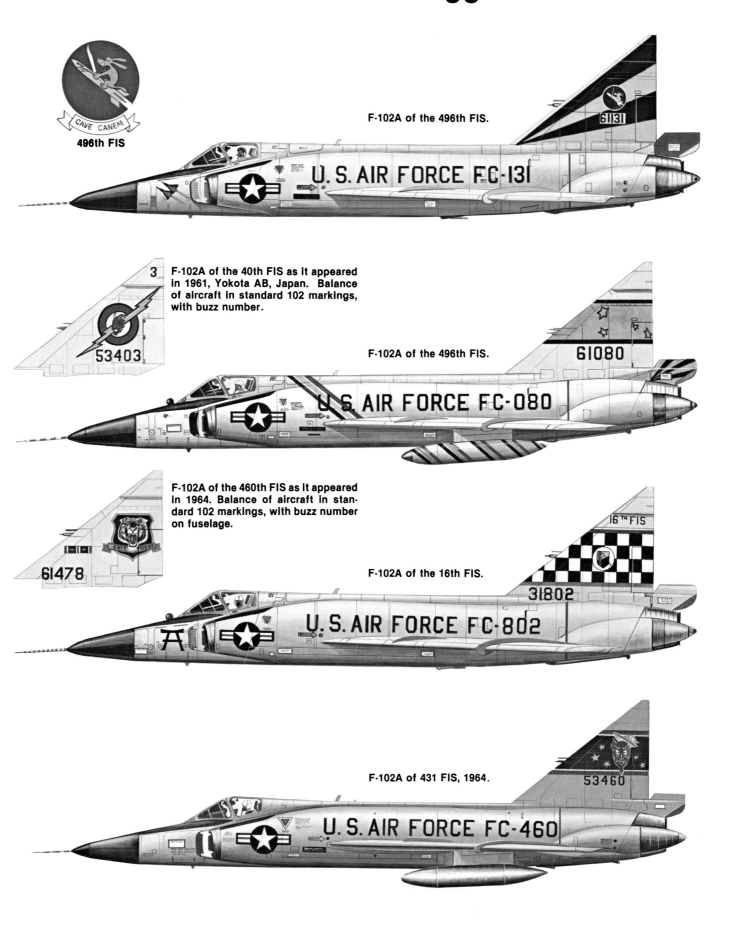

496th FIS

F-102A of the 496th FIS.

3

F-102A of the 40th FIS as it appeared in 1961, Yokota AB, Japan. Balance of aircraft in standard 102 markings, with buzz number.

F-102A of the 496th FIS.

F-102A of the 460th FIS as it appeared in 1964. Balance of aircraft in standard 102 markings, with buzz number on fuselage.

F-102A of the 16th FIS.

F-102A of 431 FIS, 1964.

One of the first F-102s to be delivered to an operational squadron, the 327th FIS at George AFB, California, is shown in August 1956. (USAF)

F-102A-35-CO at the Oklahoma City National Air Show in September 1954. Checkerboard on the tail is red, striped on fuselage are, from front: red, white, blue, yellow. Insignia on tail is that of the 327th FIS, the first unit to equip with the F-102A. (Dean Englehardt via Paul Stevens)

Early production F-102 with the taller fin, but still without modified intakes and enlarged speed brakes. (General Dynamics)

The first TF-102A was rolled out in October 1955. (USAF)

This YF is labeled YF-102C, though no formal record of a C designation seems to exist. (AAHS)

Final production configuration for the F-102A included redesigned air intakes with splitter plates which enabled the Deuce to reach Mach 1.5 and a larger speed brake. Production aircraft were returned to the San Diego plant to receive these updates, plus the complete MG-10 Fire Control System which also had data link, enabling it to interface with SAGE (Semi-Active Ground Environment). (General Dynamics)

Delta Daggers of the 175th FIS, South Dakota ANG. Red lightning bolts on fin leading edges. They later added another bolt of about the same length under the serial number. (USAF)

F-102A of the 11th FIS. Fuselage stripes are dayglo orange. (Dave Menard)

F-102A of the 4780th Air Defense Wing. White stripe on tail with red (top) and blue deltas. 192 gallon drop tanks are natural metal. (Ken Buchanan)

The 317th and 31st FIS were stationed at Elmendorf AFB, Alaska in 1958 as a part of NORAD's defenses against over-the-pole bomber attacks. (USAF)

F-102A of the 496th FIS at Hahn AB, Germany, 1961. Fuselage and drop tank stripes are blue, yellow, red. Tail stripe and speed brakes are yellow, with black outline, stripes and stars. (G. Pennick via Geer)

ADELANTO, an F-102A of the 329th FIS as it appeared at Sheppard AFB, Texas, September 1960. (Merle Olmstead via Paul Stevens)

F-102A of 32nd FIS, Soesterberg AB, Holland, 1963.

F-102A of the 327th FIS, George AFB, California.

F-102A Ejection Seat

Ram-Air Turbine

F-102A of the 4th FIS, as it appeared in 1962 while stationed in Japan.

F-102A-90-CO of the 175th FIS, SDANG, at Andrews AFB, Md. May 1964. At about this time F-102s were fitted with a ball-like IR sensor in front of the windscreen. (Robert T. O'Dell via Paul Stevens)

F-102A of the 496th FIS. Yellow tail with black stripes, speed brake appears to be dark insignia blue. Stripes on nose yellow and black, while radome is buff-colored, pitot red, white striped, missiles are red with white markings. 496th badge on both sides of tail. (Dave Menard)

The TF-102A

Since the Air Force felt that the F-102 was a handful of airplane, they didn't expect relatively inexperienced pilots to be able to fly it, without extra training. Consequently they contracted with Convair in May 1953 for a two-seater. Rather than taking the compartively simple expedient of stretching the standard airplane to make room for a tandem second seat, Convair went about the business of building a side-by-side variant. This turned out to be a great trainer, communications wise (how could you ignore the instructor if he was gesturing wildly or punching you on the arm), but a certifiable sub-sonic version of a supersonic interceptor. Not only was it not supersonic, the vast frontal area created all kinds of new aerodynamic problems. The first flight was in October 1955, but the TF was not released for performance testing for almost a year, while various combinations of fixes were tried to solve its problems. A total of 63 were built.

Massive frontal area of the TF is evident in this shot of a 157th FIS airplane at McEntire ANGB, SC, 1971. One of the canopy fixes required to combat excessive high speed buffet in the TF was installation of a row of fences on leading edge of canopy rail. (Jim Sullivan)

TF-102A at ADWC, Tyndall AFB, Florida, with camera pod under right wing and ram air turbine deployed under fuselage. (USAF)

F-102As of the Louisiana Air Guard. Blue and white stripes on tail, with 122nd FIS badge on tail (in white "V"). Top of speed brake and wing fences are red. (Paul Stevens)

F-102s of the Idaho Air National Guard's 124th FIS, Boise, Idaho. Yellow tail band and ellipse on drop tank, with black outlines and diamonds. F-102A-35-CO above was photographed in 1968 by Douglas D. Olson, while the TF at left was shot in 1966. The Deuce below was shot in 1967, the year that buzz numbers went out of favor. (via Paul Stevens)

F-102A of the 460th FIS. (Bob Burgess via Paul Stevens)

F-102A-45-CO of the 116th FIS, Washington Air Guard, Spokane, Washington, 1968. Red stripe on tail, with blue and white borders. Ace of spades is black and white, with gold stilletto with blue handle run through center. (Douglas D. Olson via Paul Stevens)

F-102A of the 64th FIS, Paine Field, Washington. Delta on tail is red, white, blue, with 64th badge in center. Wing fences are yellow, speed brakes red on 61467. (Via Jerry Geer)

F-102A-70-CO of the 111th FIS, 147th FIG, Texas ANG, Ellington AFB, Texas. Tubes for FFARs are evident in weapons bay doors. (Dr. Carlton A. Eddy via Paul Stevens)

F- and TF-102A of the 176th FIS, Wisconsin Air Guard, Truax Field, 1971. Note that an American Airlines decal has been placed over the National Guard insignia on the TF's tail, an obvious reference to the source of the Air Guard's manning requirements. (Paul Stevens)

F-102-90-CO of the 123rd FIS, Oregon Air Guard, 1968. Lightning bolt and fuselage stripes are gold (metallic) trimmed in green. (Douglas D. Olson via Paul Stevens)

F-102A-45-CO of the 186th FIS, Montana Air Guard, Great Falls, 1968. Blue tail band, with white border and stars. Stripe on fuselage and wing fences are red. (Douglas D. Olson via Paul Stevens)

F-102A-50-CO of the 118th FIS, Connecticut ANG "Flying Yankees", Bradley Field, CT, 1969. (Thomas S. Cuddy II via Paul Stevens)

TF-102A-26-CO of the Hooligans, at Elmendorf AFB, Alaska in 1969. (Norman E. Taylor via Stevens)

F-102A-55-CO of the 178th FIS, North Dakota Air Guard. Bright red tail stripe, with black border, red wing fences. The Happy Hooligans have flown a variety of interceptors, all in the ADC business, in the past two decades and always with the same markings. (Douglas D. Olson, via Paul Stevens)

F-102A-60-CO of the 147th FIG, Texas Air Guard, 1968. (Thomas S. Cuddy II via Stevens)

TF-102A of the 182nd FIS, San Antonio, Texas ANG. Distinguished Unit Citation and ANG Sticker on tail. Photographed at McEntire ANGB, S.C in 1969, shortly after transfer to the S.C. Air Guard (Jim Sullivan)

F-102A-70-CO of the 317th FIS, Elmendorf AFB, Alaska, 1968. High visibility red on tail and wing tips, with Alaskan Air Command Badge on right side of fin, 21st Composite Wing badge on left side, 317th badge on both sides of nose, Distinguished Unit Citation over national insignia on both sides of fuselage. Flashes on tanks are red. (Norman E. Taylor via Jerry Geer)

TF-102A of the 4780th ADW, at Perrin AFB, Texas, 1969. (Jerry Geer)

F-102A belonging to the Wing Commander (So it says on the drop tank!) of the 4780th ADW, Perrin AFB, TX, 1969. (Jerry Geer)

F-102A-45-CO of the 196th FIS, California Air Guard, at Elmendorf AFB, Alaska, 1969. Tail band is blue, with white stars and Air National Guard insignia in center. (Norman E. Taylor via Stevens

F-102A of the 157th FIS, South Carolina Air Guard landing at McEntire ANGB in 1968. Tail stripe is dark blue, with red and white borders. In addition to the drag chute, the 102 uses its large wing area for aerodynamic braking, the pilot holding the nose off for as long as possible. (Jim Sullivan)

F-102A at Da Nang AB, RVN, 1964. The Duece was flown by two PACAF Squadrons, the 82nd and the 509th. It was used in Vietnam for point defence of air bases and, to my knowledge, never fired a shot in anger. (USAF)

F-102s of the 509th FIS at Da Nang, 1964. Tiger on nose on 144 in standard tiger colors. PACAF badge both sides of tail. (USAF)

A three-ship in air show formation over the delta in 1966. (USAF)

(Above Left) At Tan Son Nhut, December 1965. (USAF)

Standing alert, in camouflage, at Udorn RTAB in 1969. (USAF)

F/TF-102 Aircraft Marking Specification

MARKING	LOCATION	SIZE	FS COLOR NO.
A U.S. AIR FORCE	Both sides of fuselage	Letters 21" high	15044
B Model Designation, Acft S/N and Fuel Requirement	Left side of fuselage	Letters and numbers 1" high	17036
C National Star	Both sides of fuselage	30" star	Background border - 15044
D	On under surface of right wing and top surface of left wing	40" star	Stars and Bars- 17875, Stripes 11136
E USAF	Top surface of right wing and under surface of left wing	30" high letters	15044
F Call Numbers	Both sides of vertical stabilizer	12" high numbers	17038
G Arctic Markings	One inch clearance around all large insignia and lettering		12197
H Anti-Glare	Top fuselage in front of cockpit		37038

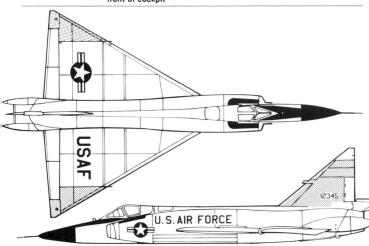

Standard USAF Camouflage

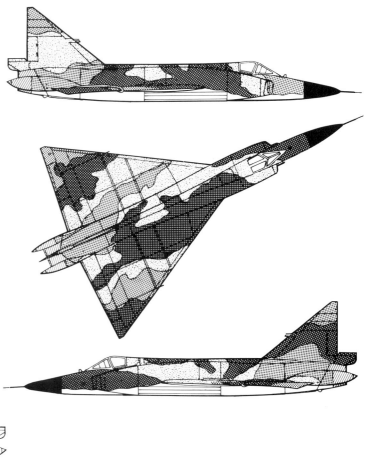

F-104 Starfighter

"The Missile with a Man in It" may not seem like a very futuristic or even unusual nickname to hang onto a fighter aircraft today, what with missiles with men in them being a more or less accepted fact of life. But back in the early 'fifties the only missiles we had were strictly experimental and had a way of blowing up in spectacular and unplanned fashion. Putting a man into a missile seemed like a really dicey proposition.....maybe a good way of creating instant aviation martyrs. So the Starfighter's nickname should be appreciated for what it meant, or implied, when the name first got hung on Lockheed's sleek and dangerous 1950s lightweight.

The Starfighter is one of those rare examples of the fighter pilot getting exactly what he asked for in an airplane. It was the direct result of a trip to Korea by its designer, Kelly Johnson, *paterfamilias* of Lockheed's famed "Skunk Works". Johnson traveled to Korea in 1952, ostensibly to get a first hand report on how his earlier brainchild, the F-80 Shooting Star, was doing in combat. American fighter pilots, though they were enjoying a ten-to-one advantage in kills over their communist rivals, continually bemoaned the fact that the nimble MiG-15 could outclimb and outturn anything they had. Johnson was impressed with their pleas for an interceptor that would beat anything the communists had. The Air Force was also impressed and they gave Lockheed a contract for two prototypes, which they designated **XF-104** and Lockheed called Model 83 "Starfighter".

Lockheed had settled on their preliminary design by March 1953. The Air Force specification called for a Mach 2 airplane that would have a combat ceiling of 60,000 feet. Johnson aimed at Mach 2.2 with a ceiling considerably higher, in an airplane that weighed in at between 15,000 and 18,000 pounds. He also wanted to use the new powerplant under development by General Electric for use in the B-58. This was the J-79, destined to become the most successful engine of the 'sixties and 'seventies. Even though a production version of the J-79 would not be available until 1956, its promised performance was so impressive that Lockheed decided to await its arrival. In the meantime, the two prototype **XF-104s** would be powered by Wright J-65s, rated at 10,200 lbs. thrust.

The prototype configuration was evolved through the use of the high speed wind tunnel at NACA Ames Lab and with a modified Convair CV-240. The CV-240 carried a computer which could be programmed to duplicate control responses of various aircraft configurations. Using these two new tools, Lockheed was able to try over 300 different variations of the main theme before settling on the final prototype configuration.

An interesting sidelight to the F-104 production program is the fact that once the basic design had been proven and approved for production, Lockheed launched an intensive study to completely redesign the way in which the 104 was built. This was done without changing the design but, in effect, completely changing the airplane. The result made the F-104 easier to mass-produce and, based on a production run of 2,500 airplanes, would save up to $12,000 per airplane. First flight of the XF-104 took place on March 4, 1954, with Tony LeVier at the controls. Throughout the rest of 1954 and 1955, LeVier, Herman "Fish" Salmon and Joe Ozier explored the XF-104's characteristics. There was plenty to explore and the test program was anything but dull, as pitch-up and roll-coupling presented problems that would have to be overcome before service acceptance.

General Electric had the first YJ-79-GE-3 engine qualified in time for insertion into the first **YF-104**, which rolled out in December 1955. First flight was made on February 17,1956 by Fish Salmon. The YF-104 was noticeably longer than the XF, having to accomodate the larger engine and additional fuel. It also had modified intakes, with a large shock cone centered on the fuselage. This modification led to some laughable efforts by the Department of Defense to classify its details. Laughable because literally thousands of people at Edwards, Burbank and Palmdale had seen the airplane and knew what the intakes looked like. But, when Lockheed wanted to officially announce the airplane to the press, DOD insisted the intakes be covered. Lockheed came up with some slick polished aluminum covers that looked for all the world like a part of the airplane, even though it was obvious they couldn't be anything other than what they were.....fake.

The first XF-104 in flight over Edwards AFB, in 1954. Even with the temporarily installed J-65 engine, which developed only 10,500 lbs. thrust with afterburner, the XF-104 reached a speed of Mach 1.6, which made it the fastest of the Century Series up to that time. This photo was captioned "the first official view of the XF-104", but carries later markings. (USAF)

(In previous pictures, Lockheed had managed to conceal the intakes by placing one of their better looking employees in the foreground, concealing the strategic parts of the airplane.) The intake covers became known as "Flight Falsies".

Lockheed received an order for 155 **F-104As** in 1955, all for the Air Defense Command. One of the YFs reached Mach 2 in April 1956. There was absolutely no denying the potential of the 104. In fact, the airframe would obviously go much faster than the engine could stand to push it. (The red-line was put at 2.2 because of inlet temperature limitations on the engine.) Though the Starfighter was a really amazing piece of work, it was also very troublesome. The test program lasted four years and involved the first 52 airplanes. When service acceptance was finally achieved in January 1958, it was relatively short-lived. The first squadron to operate the 104 was the 83rd FIS at Hamilton AFB, California. The early F-104s all had a downward ejection seat, primarily because it was felt that the available methods of seat propulsion were insufficient to get the seat high enough, fast enough, to clear the tail. This seat might have been acceptable if an ejection at altitude could be guaranteed. Unfortunately, a larger percentage of ejections seemed to come close to the ground, on takeoff or landings. The only way to kill yourself more quickly than riding a crippled, uncontrollable airplane into the ground is to blast yourself into the ground through the bottom of the airplane. The service 104s were grounded in April 1958. The grounding was because of some problems that had developed with the new J-79 engine. Those problems were eventually ironed out and the 104 was once again cleared for flight. Later that year Lockheed came out with the C-2 seat, the first upward ejecting model to be fitted to the 104. Throughout the test program, and much of its service life, the 104 has maintained the worst safety record of any of the Century Series. Far worse than any of the fighters that have been developed since. It was simply not a forgiving airplane. If you made a mistake, it would very likely be the last one you made in that airplane!

Korea was the last real eyeball to eyeball airwar. Oh sure, there was plenty of air combat in Vietnam, but the bad guys were almost always under ground control. In the Korean air war, fighter airspeeds had increased by approximately 50% from WW II. Guns were still the primary armament and you still had to see the other guy first, then close to within a few hundred yards at most before shooting. Nobody knew what would happen when fighter airspeeds went up by 300%. For that matter, probably not too many people anticipated that happening within just a few years. What happened was that the airframe/engine combination ran away from the pilot's ability to see and think without electronic help. Unfortunately, the age of miniturazation had not arrived and there was no radar that was both strong enough and small enough to fit into the 104.

Lockheed soon realized that they would never recover the cost of developing the 104 if they had to rely on sales to USAF. (The ADC airplanes were withdrawn from service in 1959 and turned over to the Air National Guard.) They promptly set their sights on Europe. To their credit, they were open-minded enough, and innovative enough, to realize that they could not hope to sell "made in America" American airplanes to Europeans. They also realized that our NATO allies would need multi-mission aircraft. So began yet another redesign of the 104.

The redesign of the 104 actually began in 1956. The only noticeable change from the 104A was the larger, boosted rudder, which had been introduced on the first two seat 104, the **F-104B.** Internally, though, it was considerably changed. Not only had the structure been strengthened to accomodate the high "Q" ground attack mission, but a new and more sophisticated set of avionics had been installed. The Autonetics F-15A NASARR (North American Search And Ranging Radar) provided for enhanced air-to-air capability, as well as radar bombing and terrain avoidance capability. The intakes were anti-iced, bigger tires and brake chute were fitted, an autopilot, an inertial navigation set, an infra-red sight and provisions for carrying 2,000 lbs. of stores on the centerline and 1,500 lbs. on each of four wing stations was made. With all of these improvements, in the hands of an experienced fighter pilot, the 104 need not take a back seat to any fighter in the world. Unfortunately, the redesigned Starfighter was not destined to be placed in the hands of experienced fighter pilots.

The Germans needed the 104 for more than just defense. They needed it (or something like it) to rebuild a whole industry. The vital German aviation industry, from which most of the dynamic new ideas

This photo shows the early test markings for the XF-104 and is believed to have been taken in July 1954 at Edwards. (USAF)

of the '40s had sprung, had lain dormant since the end of World War II. Now, in an effort to rebuild, the Bundesrepublik went all out to get a modern and sopohisticated weapons system they could build in their factories. Lockheed was willing and able to provide them with that system and, though the operational history of the 104 in the Bundesluftwaffe was one disaster after another, the program did indeed resurrect the German aerospace industry.

The Germans had signed their contract to license-build the 104 in March 1959. Their lead was quickly followed by Canada in September, Japan in January 1960, Holland in April, Belgium in June, and Italy in March 1961. The F-104 became the largest international manufacturing program in history and led to the sale of the 104 to several other countries, making it the most widely used interceptor in the world during the 'sixties.

"The Missile with a Man in It" remains somewhat of an enigma today. Experienced fighter pilots will swear by it, but there is no denying that it prevented hundreds of other pilots from gaining any additional experience. It was a record breaker in the 'fifties. Pilots of the 83rd FIS gained world's records for speed and altitude in 1958. It was the first time that these records had been established with the same type aircraft. And there is evidence that it might still be a record-holder, given more favorable circumstances. Darryl Greenamayer's RB-104 "Red Baron" did establish a new closed course speed record in 1976, hitting 1,010 mph. Unfortunately, the "official" monitoring equipment malfunctioned and the RB-104 was destroyed in a later accident before another record attempt could be made.

The second YF-104A at Edwards in 1956 with the now famous "flight falsies" in place covering the intakes. The leading edges of the wings were so sharp (with a radius of 16/1000) that covers are installed on the ground to keep ground crew from injuring themselves. One advantage of the super-thin wings and stabilator is the fact that ice will not adhere to leading edges. (USAF)

F-104G/J

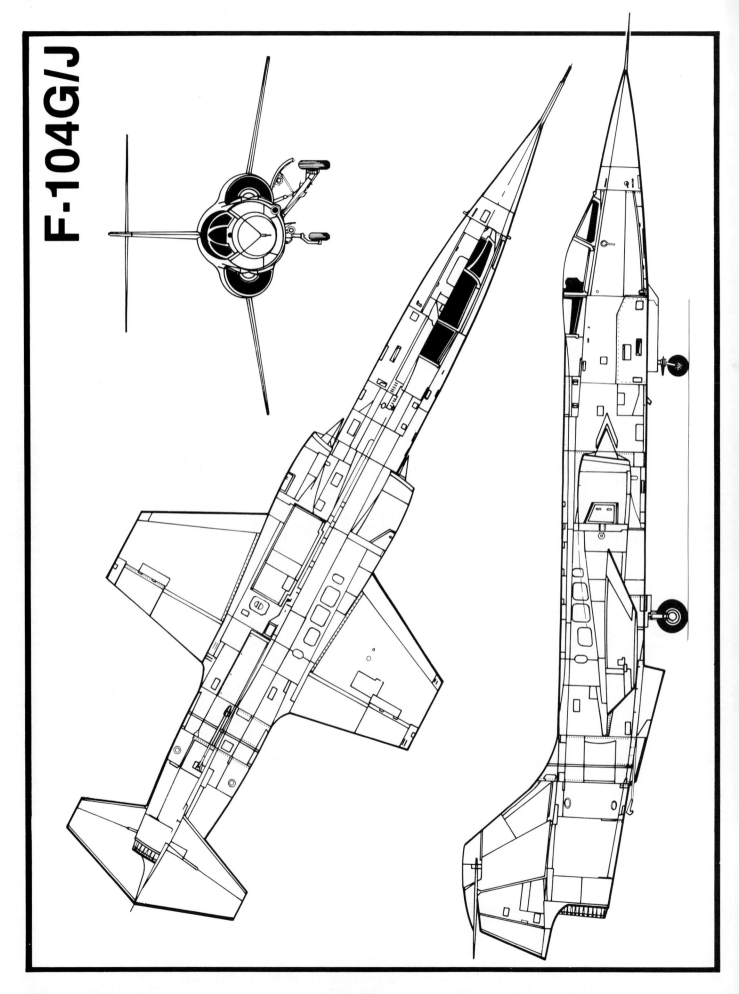

F-104As of the 83rd FIS over the Golden Gate Bridge in 1958. (USAF)

(Below Right) F-104A-16-LO of the Arizona Air Guard, 1964. The ventral fin was fitted to the last of the YFs to increase the lateral stability at high speed. It does double duty, acting also as an antenna. (Paul Stevens)

F-104A of the 83rd FIS, with Squadron markings applied, in 1959. Though the operational force of Starfighters was grounded in 1958, pilots of the 83rd used test aircraft to set new altitude (91,249 ft) and speed (1,404 mph) records in May of that year. (Douglas D. Olson via Paul Stevens)

The first of the two seat versions, the F-104B. The B was first flown on February 7, 1957. It was to be used strictly for training and transition and had the cannon and some fuselage fuel capacity removed to make room for the second seat. 26 were built, all by Lockheed. (Peter Bowers via Jim Sullivan)

F-104A-25-LO of the 157th FIS, South Carolina Air Guard, 1963. (Paul Stevens)

F-104A-25-LO of the 337th FIS, 1960. Highly polished natural metal fuselage, white wings. Rear fuselage sections are titanium. (David Lucabagh via Paul Stevens)

F-104A of the 319th FIS, early '60s. Overall light grey, white wings, natural metal rear fuselage sections. (David Menard)

The first of the C models appeared in 1958. 77 were built for USAF's Tactical Air Command. Primary differences from the A included provision for aerial refueling, larger and more powerful J-79-GE-7 engine, blown flaps and provision for air-to-ground stores capability.

Two non-standard F-104 instrument panels (center panel contains special test instrumentation). Later 104 models would have the radar scope in the lower center of the panel, while the balance would be similar. These photos released in 1960 illustrate the relative simplicity of the 104 in the day fighter mission. (USAF)

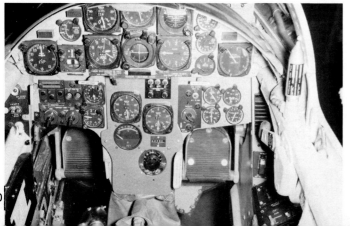

(Right and Below) F-104Cs of TAC's 479th TFW, based at George AFB, California, 1963, shown here during Operation Swift Strike III, a joint Army-Air Force maneuver held in the Carolinas in July 1963. Starfighters operated out of Myrtle Beach AFB. (USAF and Duane Kasulka via Jerry Geer)

(Below Right) F-104Cs were eventually turned over the Puerto Rico Air Guard when the 479th TFW re-equipped with the Phantom in 1965. PRANG flew Starfighters until their retirement in 1975. (Lionel Paul via Jim Sullivan)

The NF-104 was operated by USAF's Aerospace Research Pilots School at Edwards AFB. Three were built, the modifications including the addition of 2 feet of span to each wing, LR-121/AR-2 rocket engine under tail, HTP reaction controls (for pitch and yaw in nose, and for roll in each of the wings) and modified intake shock cones to accomodate higher speeds. They were used to train pilots for lifting body flights, X-15 missions and eventually the Space Shuttle. One was lost when Chuck Yeager got it into a flat spin and rode it down from over 100,000 feet to 8,000 before finally giving up and punching out. Yeager was badly burned, but survived. The RCS control handle is mounted on the left center of the panel. (USAF)

NASA has operated the F-104 for several years. In the pre-PR-oriented era, their aircraft were natural metal with yellow and blue flashes (1966). In later years they acquired a much flashier scheme of white, dark and light blues, with gold stripes separating the colors. The yellow fin flash was retained. (USAF and Peter Mancus via Jim Sullivan)

In 1959 24 F-104As were converted to QF-104 Drones. They have been operated by Air Force Systems Command. (USAF)

Although they carry USAF markings, these F-104Gs are owned by the Federal Republic of Germany. All German Starfighter pilots are trained by USAF instructors at Luke AFB, Arizona. German 104s at Luke are maintained by Lockheed Service Company, under a civilian contract awarded by USAF. Germany pays approximated $27 million annually for these services (USAF)

F-104G of Jabo G 33 at Florennes, Belgium, September 1972. The first of the 'G' models flew on October 5, 1960. First German-built Starfighter was delivered in August 1961, and the first Luftwaffe unit to equip with the Starfighter was Jabo G 31 at Norvenich. Germany's troubles with the Starfighter led to its being grounded on several occasions, causing national furor to equal Watergate in the US. Other NATO countries have not had the problems that Germany had. (Udo Weiss via Jim Sullivan)

(Above Right) RF-104G of AG-52, 1969. The reconnaissance version has the cannon deleted and three cameras installed in their place. Modifications for the RF-104 were done at Avio Diepen at Ypenburg. (Dave Menard)

TF-104G of MFG-2 at Royal Flush XVIII, Bremgarten, June 1975. The West German Navy did not experience the loss rates of the Luftwaffe with its 104s. (Gunter Grondstein)

CF-104G of the Royal Canadian Air Force at RAF Alconbury, 1967. Canadian Starfighters were optimized for the strike fighter role. They were assigned to NATO's Number 1 Air Division during the mid-sixties. The first Canadian unit to equip with the CF-104 was No. 427 Squadron at Zweibrucken in December 1962. (Dave Menard via Paul Stevens)

(Right) Lockheed built 38 CF-104Ds for Canada. (Gunter Grondstein)

(Bottom Right) CF-104G in overall dark green camouflage, white tail with red maple leaf for Tactical Air Meet, Wildenrath AB, Germany, June 1978. (Gunter Grondstein)

(Below) Canadian Starfighters have carried a wide variety of camouflage schemes during their service life. This particular version is in RAF grey and dark green, with low visibility national markings (red maple leaf on blue circle, flag on tail is all red with no background). (Gunter Grondstein)

F-104J of the 205th Squadron, 6th Wing, JASDF, Komatsu ABA, Japan, 1979. The Starfighter is license manufactured in Japan by Mitsubishi and Kawasaki. The first 3 F-104Js were built by Lockheed and first flew in June 1961. They were then disassembled, shipped to Japan and reassembled by Mitsubishi. Japanese Starfighters are optimized for the air-to-air role, in keeping with their "defense only" treaty. The first Japanese units to get the 104 were the 201st and 202nd Squadrons at Chitose and Nyutabaru. The Japanese name for the 104 is *Eiko* (Glory), a name that can be appreciated by those that fly the 104. (Shinichi Ohtaki)

(Left) Italy is one of the largest (if least publicized) operators and builders of the F-104. Italian 104s were built by a group comprised of Fiat, Aerfer, Macchi, SIAI-Marchetti, Piaggio and SACA. They built the most up-to-date version of the 104, the S model, so named because it is capable of carrying the radar-guided Sparrow missile. (Michel C. Klaver)

Early Dutch camouflage scheme was overall light grey. (Michel C. Klaver)

RF-104G of 306 Squadron, Royal Netherlands Air Force (KLu) at Ypenberg, Netherlands, 1970, curiously marked. Among the markings are a German cross behind the national insignia (a war-games kill?), outline paintings of a giraffe (over the numeral '2' of the serial) and a victory cup (under the windscreen) plus a star, a Canadian flag and two bird's footprints. (Russell-Smith via Jim Sullivan)

(Left) TF-104G of RNAF Operational Conversion Unit. The Dutch operated 5 squadrons of the 104, two interceptor, two fighter-bomber and one recconnaissance. (Michel C. Klaver)

(Right) The Belgian Air Force got the 104 in 1965. They operated four squadrons of 104s, 23 and 31 at Kleine Brogel and 349 and 350 at Beauvechain. Belgian 104s were overall natural metal with light grey nose and white wings, until receiving their camouflage in the late '60s. (Michel C. Klaver)

(Right) The Belgian Air Force received a total of 189 Starfighters, 188 of which were manufactured by SABCA at Gosselies. They eventually adopted a camouflage scheme of 14064 dark green, 14102 light green, and 20219 tan, with 26622 light grey undersurfaces, as shown on these 104s of 10 FBW at TAM 78. (Michel C. Klaver and Gunter Grondstein)

F-102A of 176th FIS, Wisconsin ANG as it appeared at
William Tell Competition, Tyndall AFB, Fla., 1972.

F-102A of 112th Fighter Interceptor Group,
Pennsylvania ANG, 1978.

F-102A 118th FIS, Connecticut ANG.

**Air National
Guard Insignia**

F-102A of the 190th FIS, 124th FIG, Idaho
ANG, Boise, 1975.

Norway has operated one squadron of Starfighters, No. 331 at Bodo. Camouflage schemes have ranged from dark olive overall to painted aluminum in recent years. (Michel C. Klaver and Gunter Grondstein)

Formation of Starfighters of Ejercito Del Aire, Squadron 104, operating from Torrejon AB, Spain. (Salvador Mafe-Huertas)

F-104 Aircraft Marking Specification

	MARKING	LOCATION	SIZE	FS COLOR NO.
A	U.S. AIR FORCE	Both sides of fuselage	Letters 13" high	15044
B	Model Designation, Acft S/N and fuel Requirement	Left side of fuselage	Letters and numbers 1" high	17038
C	National Star	Both sides of fuselage	30" star	Background border - 15044, Stars and Bars - 17875, Stripes 11136
D		On under surface of right wing and top surface of left wing	30" star	
E	USAF	Top surface of right wing and under surface of left wing	30" high letters	15044
F	Call Numbers	Both sides of vertical stabilizer	12" high numbers	17038
G	Arctic Markings	One inch clearance around all large insignia and lettering		12197
H	Anti-Glare	Top of fuselage in front of cockpit		37038

Standard USAF Camouflage

"Asia Minor" Camouflage

The first YF-105A is taxied out for its first flight by Republic's chief test pilot, Russell M. "Rusty" Roth, on October 22, 1955. On this flight he pushed the YF-105A through the sound barrier, to Mach 1.2. (USAF)

F-105 Thunderchief

Of all the Centruy Series, the F-105 is the airplane that I regard as being the most heroic. In its early career, the Thunderchief suffered the fate of most aircraft which carry the "F" designator but do not live up the the image of the fighter as conceived by most fighter pilots. (It has been my experience that fighter pilots think of themselves as clear air mass, G-pulling, one-on-one dogfighters first, and "mud movers"....bomb droppers....second.) The F-105 was designed as a long range strike fighter. Had the Air Force adopted the "A" (Attack) designator 20 years sooner, it might have become the first of the "A" series. As it was, the fighter appellation only served to garner the 105 some uncomplimentary nicknames, such as "Lead Sled", "Ultra Hog" (the F-84 series had been named "Hog" and "Super Hog") and "ThunderThud". It took a real war to demonstrate the "Thud", as it became known, was perhaps the most successful of the Century Series in combat.

The F-105 was born on the drawing boards at Farmingdale as a result of a desire to improve upon the performance of the F-84. The improvement program developed into a completely new design, a design whose merits convinced Republic Aviation that they had something worth pursuing as a private venture. The embryo design, then known in company parlance as Advanced Project 63, was submitted to the Department of Defense in March 1952. DOD liked what it saw and six months later a contract for tooling and engineering was awarded.

If the initial favorable reaction of DOD had encouraged Republic to think that they had a relatively smooth road ahead for their new design, subsequent events would change their outlook considerably. A month after contract award, the engine specification was changed from the Allison J-71 to the then red-hot Pratt & Whitney J-57. In March 1953, Republic was given an order for 37 **XF-105AOs**. When the armistice was signed in Korea in July, the predictable rush to disarm claimed the 105 program as a probable victim....unless, of course, the 105 could be integrated into the future strategic picture somehow. Small, inconclusive wars such as Korea just would not be popular in the future, everyone thought. It was far better to heed the sage advice of Teddy Roosevelt. And our nuclear strike forces would be the big stick that went along with the soft talk of the Eisenhower years.

The folks at Farmingdale got the message. The F-105 became the most powerful single-engine, single pilot airplane the world had ever seen. The mock-up, which was unveiled in October 1953 revealed a long range, high speed bomber that could carry its nuclear payload in a bomb bay that was larger than that of a B-17. Once again DOD sat up and took notice. Things looked pretty good again....for the moment.

In February 1954 the bottom fell out, again. DOD cut its order from 37 to 15 airplanes. Numerous vacillations followed. Pratt & Whitney J-75s were specified in place of the J-57s. In September the order was cut to 3 airplanes. In October it was increased to 6. In February 1955, the order was again set at 15, with allowance for the original 37 incorporated in the fiscal '56 budget. But before Republic was allowed to go ahead with the full order, they were told that the F-105 would have to win a competitive evaluation against the North American F-107. The **YF-105A**, which had first flown on October 22, 1955, won the competitive evaluations handily. Still DOD procrastinated and the decision to put the Thunderchief into production was delayed until January 1957.

The first operational 105s were delivered to the 335th Tactical Fighter Squadron on May 26, 1958. They were **F-105B** models. The 335th got 18 of them. The 335th would do a large share of the weapons system testing while stationed at Eglin AFB, Florida, which had the largest range complex of any US air base. The balance of the 4th TFW, the 334th,336th and 333rd TFSs were stationed at Seymour-Johnson AFB. The 334th and 336th also got Bs, while the 333rd became the first to get the newer **F-105D** model. The entire 4th TFW eventually got the D model, and the Bs went to the New Jersey Air Guard.

With the advent of the D model, TAC could nearly claim a measure of parity with SAC. They had a long range strike bomber, which was unquestionably faster and more manueverable than anything SAC had. It was equipped with a Doppler Navigation System, the Thunderstick Fire Control System which included radar and toss bomb computer and the more powerful dash 19 version of the J-75 which developed 26,000 lbs. of thrust in afterburner. The plan was to equip 14 Wings with the Thunderchief, which would have meant a production run of at least 1,500 airplanes.

Unfortunately, the new Kennedy Administration saw things in a different light than had the Eisenhower Administration. One can only guess at the motivation of these men when they decided that the American armed forces must be equipped to fight Korean type wars instead of one cataclysmic, decisive, and probably final war. It could be that the young President felt he must be able to demonstrate some willingness to use American arms, short of nuclear holocaust, or that the Russsians would challenge democracies with brushfire wars which would have to be put out as they erupted. Whatever the reason, the direction of American strategy underwent an abrupt swerve in the direction of conventional warfare in the early 1960s. The long range strike fighter that had undergone the metamorphosis to a strategic weapon (and was only beginning to be appreciated for its potential) was now thought to be too restricted in its ability to adapt to this new strategy. This assessment could not have been farther from the truth, but that did not become apparent until after the production lines had shut down in 1964, after having produced 833 F-105s.

F-104 Starfighter

F-104A of the 151st FIS, 134th FIG, Tennessee Air National Guard.

6085I
FG-851
TENN AIR GUARD

QF-104A-1-LO Drone, operated by Air Force Systems Command in the early 1960s.

60736
QFG-736
U.S. AIR FORCE

Full pressure suit, as worn in late fifties, especially for publicity shot of the "Missile with a Man in It." (F-104)

F-104 Optical Gunsight

F-104G of MFG-2. Bundesmarine.

MARINE
26 + 75

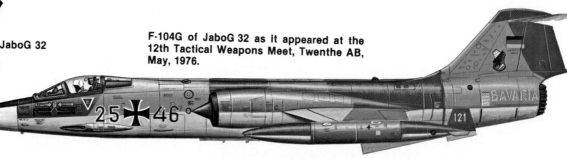

JaboG 32

F-104G of JaboG 32 as it appeared at the 12th Tactical Weapons Meet, Twenthe AB, May, 1976.

BAVARIA
25 + 46
121

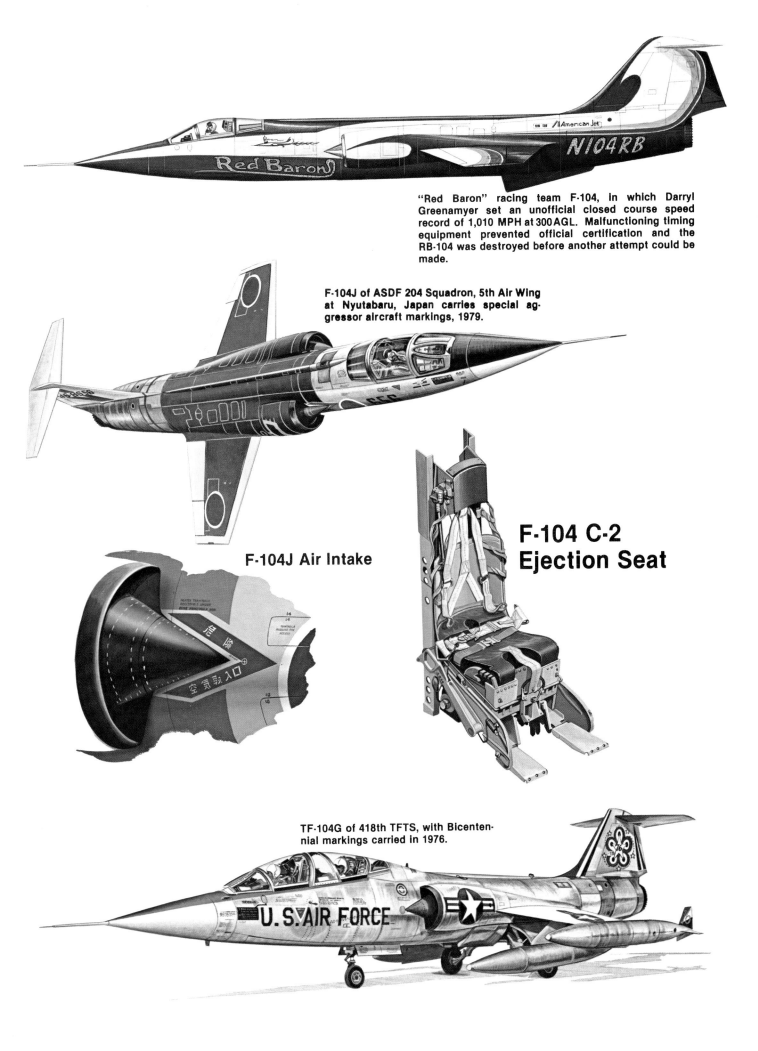

"Red Baron" racing team F-104, in which Darryl Greenamyer set an unofficial closed course speed record of 1,010 MPH at 300 AGL. Malfunctioning timing equipment prevented official certification and the RB-104 was destroyed before another attempt could be made.

F-104J of ASDF 204 Squadron, 5th Air Wing at Nyutabaru, Japan carries special aggressor aircraft markings, 1979.

F-104 C-2 Ejection Seat

F-104J Air Intake

TF-104G of 418th TFTS, with Bicentennial markings carried in 1976.

The third of four F-105B-1-REs at Edwards in June 1958. Note that the "straight" intakes have been replaced with the forward swept intake lips and that the window behind the canopy is retained. (USAF)

The last of 45 F-105D-6-REs at Eglin AFB for ordnance tests. Circles on fuselage and vertical fin are for chase plane camera calibration. Ordnance carried is BLU-11/B Fire Bombs (Napalm). (Republic)

(Below Left) F-105B-10-RE loaded with practice bombs. The window behind the cockpit has been abandoned. This is typical pre-1960s markings scheme of natural metal overall, with dark green (37038) antiglare panel, TAC badge on tail. (Republic)

Early F-105D of the 4th TFW carried Indian head insignia on nose, along with white-edged green band. (USAF)

F-105D

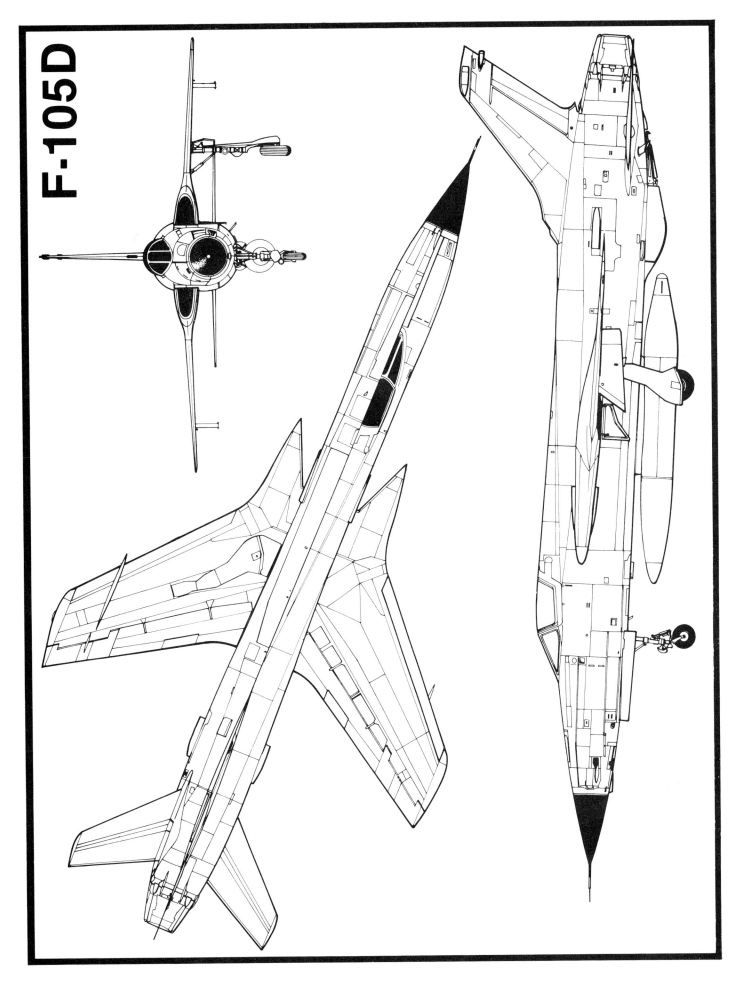

F-105 Thunderchief

F-105D of the 335th TFS, 4th TFW.

TAC Insignia

F-105D Refueling Probe

F-105D of the 562nd TFS, 23rd TFW, early 1960s.

F-105D of the 4th TFW.

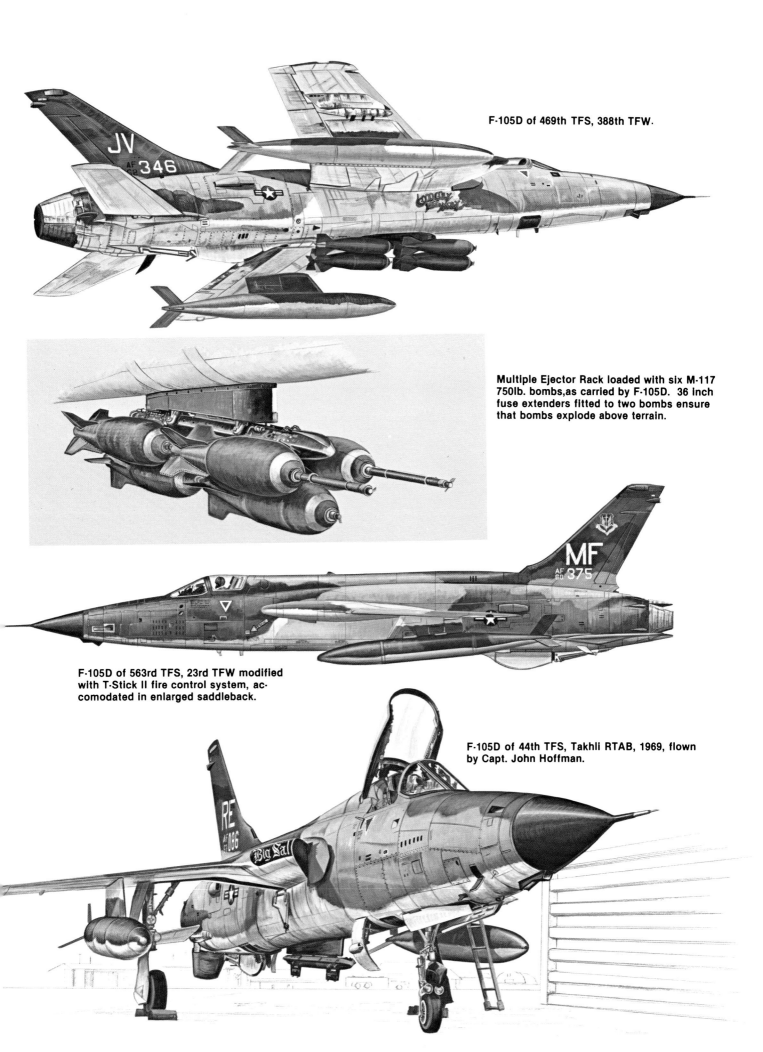

F-105D of 469th TFS, 388th TFW.

Multiple Ejector Rack loaded with six M-117 750lb. bombs, as carried by F-105D. 36 inch fuse extenders fitted to two bombs ensure that bombs explode above terrain.

F-105D of 563rd TFS, 23rd TFW modified with T-Stick II fire control system, accomodated in enlarged saddleback.

F-105D of 44th TFS, Takhli RTAB, 1969, flown by Capt. John Hoffman.

One of the more notable units to receive the F-105 was the USAF Thunderbirds Aerial Demonstration Team, which flew six shows early in the 1964 show season in the F-105B. An accident grounded the 105s and the subsequent investigation revealed the need for extensive modifications to the 105 before it could rejoin the team. TAC HQ made the decision to have the team transition to the F-100D for the balance of the 1974 season. They were to get their modified Thuds back for the 1965 season, however other operational considerations forced the Air Force to rethink that decision. The 105s that the T-birds had flown were transfered to the 141st TFS of the New Jersey Air Guard. (Republic and Geer/Pickett Collection)

F-105D-25-RE at Sioux City, Iowa airshow, 1964, in the early '60s overall aluminum-painted finish. (Paul Stevens)

F-105D-15-RE of the 49th TFW during a stop at Prestwick, Scotland enroute to the Wing's base at Spangdahlem AB, West Germany, 1964. (Geer)

F-105F-1-RE of the 8th TFW, at Kadena AB, Okinawa in 1964. Band on tail is yellow, edged black. PACAF badge on tail. (Geer)

The third from the end of the line, an F-105F, leaves Farmingdale on January 9, 1965. (Republic)

F-105Ds of the 23rd TFW, immediately prior to their deployment to Da Nang, RVN, 1965. (USAF via Menard)

F-105Ds of the 36th TFW, based at Bitburg AB, West Germany, in the early '60s (Republic)

F-105Ds with their speed brakes deployed. When the landing gear is down, top and bottom petals do not operate, since they would interfere with deployment of drag chute and normal nose-high landing attitude. (Republic)

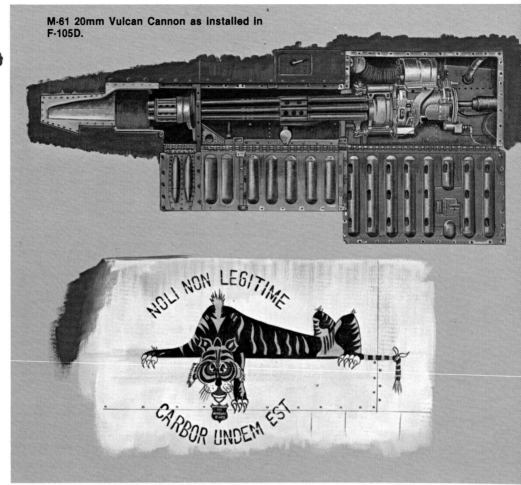

M-61 20mm Vulcan Cannon as installed in F-105D.

Typical Stenciling

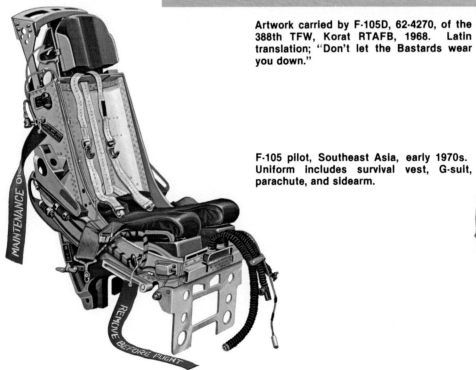

Artwork carried by F-105D, 62-4270, of the 388th TFW, Korat RTAFB, 1968. Latin translation; "Don't let the Bastards wear you down."

F-105 pilot, Southeast Asia, early 1970s. Uniform includes survival vest, G-suit, parachute, and sidearm.

F-105D Ejection Seat

F-106 Delta Dart

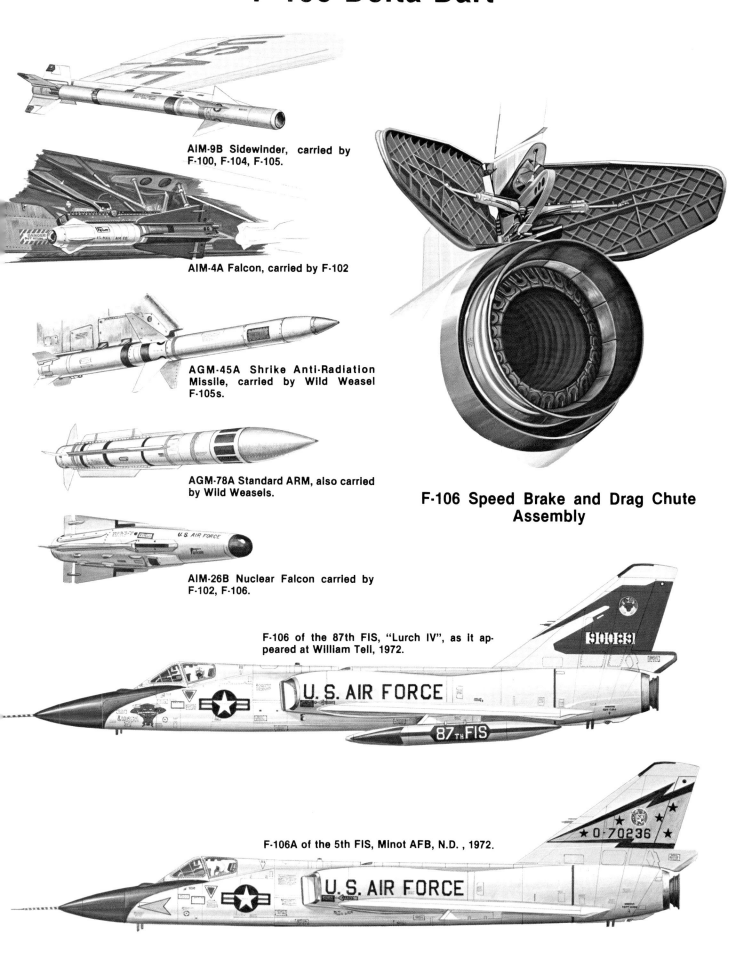

AIM-9B Sidewinder, carried by F-100, F-104, F-105.

AIM-4A Falcon, carried by F-102

AGM-45A Shrike Anti-Radiation Missile, carried by Wild Weasel F-105s.

AGM-78A Standard ARM, also carried by Wild Weasels.

AIM-26B Nuclear Falcon carried by F-102, F-106.

F-106 Speed Brake and Drag Chute Assembly

F-106 of the 87th FIS, "Lurch IV", as it appeared at William Tell, 1972.

F-106A of the 5th FIS, Minot AFB, N.D., 1972.

Miss Universe, **an F-105D-5-RE at Da Nang, 1966. (Neal Schneider via R.M. Hill)**

In 1966 the war took on a much more serious aspect, the introduction of camouflage and sprouting of ECM "lumps and bumps" on most aircraft attesting to the effectiveness of North Vietnam's anti-aircraft defenses. These 105s are shown with the favorite load for hardened or industrial targets, six 750 lb. GP bombs, as they taxi out from their base in Thailand. In spite of the loss of 60 105s in 1965 and 85 in 1966 the Thud proved itself the most effective long-range bomber in USAF service. (Republic)

The Ripper **(Left) and** Commie Stomper **(Below) were F-105Ds of the 354th TFS, 355th TFW, and flying their missions against North Vietnam from Takhli RTAB. Early in the war there was serious concern that the 105 would become extinct before the war could be won, since NVA defenses were taking a heavy toll and the production lines had shut down in 1964. The introduction of Wild Weasel flights and integration of strike forces greatly cut losses. (USAF)**

F-105F of the 44th TFS, 355th TFW. The 44th was the Wild Weasel squadron for the 355th, and its F models contained special equipment in the rear cockpit for detection and tracking of NVA SAM radars. The EWO (Electronic Warfare Officer) who manned the rear seat was more familiarly known as a "Bear". (USAF)

44th TFS Vampires F-105D about to hit the tanker, post strike. Tankers were a must for the 105s, since the high density altitudes encountered in Southeast Asia often meant they had to take off with less than a full load of fuel, then refuel enroute to the target. Fuel consumption was greatest at low altitude and at the high speeds necessary for survival over the North, which meant they needed the tankers outbound too. (USAF)

F-105F of the 44th TFS carries the names given it by two different crews, Jefferson Aireplane, and Half a yard. It is configured for a long mission, with 650 gallon centerline tank, 450 gallon wing tanks and internal fuel totaling 1450 gallons. It is armed with Shrike ARMs on outboard pylons, the standard weapon for use against SAM sites. (Col. Don Kutyna)

(Below Right) Good Vibrations a D of the 44th TFS. (Col. Don Kutyna)

Sweet Caroline, another F of the 44th TFS, armed with anti-personnel load of Mk 82 500 lb. bombs, particularly effective against SAM and radar directed gun sites. (Col. Don Kutyna)

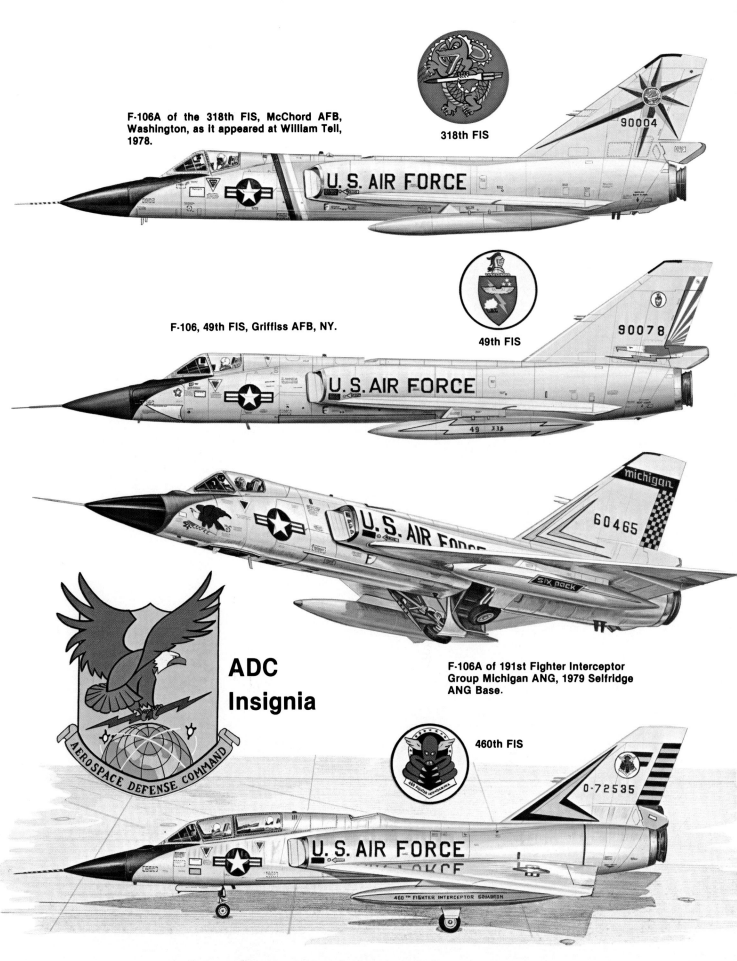

F-106A of the 318th FIS, McChord AFB, Washington, as it appeared at William Tell, 1978.

318th FIS

90004

F-106, 49th FIS, Griffiss AFB, NY.

49th FIS

90078

michigan

60465

SIX pack

ADC Insignia

AEROSPACE DEFENSE COMMAND

F-106A of 191st Fighter Interceptor Group Michigan ANG, 1979 Selfridge ANG Base.

460th FIS

0-72535

U.S. AIR FORCE

460 TH FIGHTER INTERCEPTOR SQUADRON

F-106B of the 460th FIS, McChord AFB, 1972.

The Polish Glider was the F-105D flown by Col. Don Kutyna on his combat tour with the 44th TFS. The name alludes to both the gliding properties of the Thud and to Col. Kutyna's heritage. Badge under cockpit is a gold outlined red shield, with a silver Polish eagle. Scroll under badge reads *YANKEE AIR POLACK*. (Col. Don Kutyna)

Billie Fern, an F-105-31-RE of the 354th TRS, 355th TFW, out of Takhli RTAB on the tanker over Laos, pre-strike. (Col. Don Kutyna)

The maintenance troops of the 105 Wings in Thailand had one of the most demanding jobs of the war, as their airplanes were operated for long hours in corrosive weather and at the limits of their performance much of the time. (Col. Don Kutyna)

Memphis Belle II, an F-105D-10-RE of the 357th TFS, 355th TFW carried the same pin-up as it's B-17 predecessor, and it was credited with two MIG kills. (Stars are just above Presidential Unit Citation, below windscreen in this photo.) (Col. Don Kutyna)

Armament crew loading a Shrike Anti-Radiation Missile on the outboard pylon of a Wild Weasel F-105F of the 44th TFS. (Col. Don Kutyna)

F-105D radome opened to reveal NASAAR R-14 Radar. (Col. Don Kutyna)

Four photos that prove the ability of the Thud to take it as well as it dish it out. Thud in bottom photo flew 300 miles back to its base after losing its right stabilator to groundfire. In other cases, one heat-seeking missile was often not enough to bring a 105 down and the Thud was capable of sustaining major damage to its airframe and continue to fly, as long as there was no in-flight fire to compound the problem. (USAF)

The completion of a combat tour (100 missions over North Vietnam) was occasion for celebration. This sequence of four photos shows the "parade", an impromptu procession made up of flightline vehicles, fellow pilots on the Mopeds they used to get around the base, with the Squadron C.O.'s car leading. Jim Ryder, in the *Iron Duke* had just finished his 100th. The extended refuelling probe, an elaborate variation on the extended middle digit, was displayed to fellow pilots in rude greeting. When the pilot climbed down from his airplane, the fire truck would be standing by to wet him down. This would generally be followed by champagne and a trip to the club, where the celebrant was ceremoniously thrown into the swimming pool. (Col. Don Kutyna)

F-105F of the 121st TFS, D.C. Air Guard, at Andrews AFB, Md. April 1973. (Jim Sullivan)

Survivors of the Vietnam War returned to the United States to serve with several Air National Guard Units. This F-105D-25-RE had served with the 357th TFS, 355th TFW at Takhli as *Jeanie II*, in 1970. It is shown here as it appeared in April 1976 at Byrd Field, VA, while assigned to the 149th TFS, VAANG. (Jim Sullivan)

F-105B-10-RE of the 141st TFS, N.J. ANG, as it appeared in April 1971. (Jim Sullivan)

F-105D of the 457th TFS, 301st TFW, a AFRES unit of the 10th Air Force was stationed at Carswell AFB, Texas. It is shown here during a visit to Germany. 30 Ds were retrofitted with the Thunderstick II fire control system which improved all-weather bombing accuracy up to seven times. (Gunter Grondstein)

F-105G of the 35th TFW, George AFB, California. Experience in the Vietnam War demonstrated the need for Wild Weasel dedicated squadrons and the 105G was specially equipped to carry out this mission. It is being replaced with the F-4G Wild Weasel Phantom. (Shinichi Ohtaki) (Below Right) QRC-380 ECM blisters on the fuselage of the F-105G are an integral part of the Wild Weasel mission equipment (Republic) (Below) Gun camera for the F-105D being loaded prior to mission over Vietnam. (USAF)

F-105 Aircraft Marking Specification

MARKING	LOCATION	SIZE	FS COLOR NO.
A U.S. Air Force	Both sides of fuselage	Letters 12" high	15044
B Model Designation, Acft S/N and fuel Requirement	Left side of fuselage	Letters and numbers 1" high	17038
C National Star	Both sides of fuselage	30" star	Background border -15044
D	On under surface of right wing and top surface of left wing	30" star	Stars and Bars - 17875, Stripes - 11136
E USAF	Top surface of right wing and under surface of left wing	35" high letters	15044
F Call Numbers	Both sides of vertical stalilzer	12" high numbers	17038
G Artic Markings	One inch clearance around all large insignia and lettering		12197
H Anti-Glare	Top of fuselage around cockpit		37038

Standard USAF Camouflage

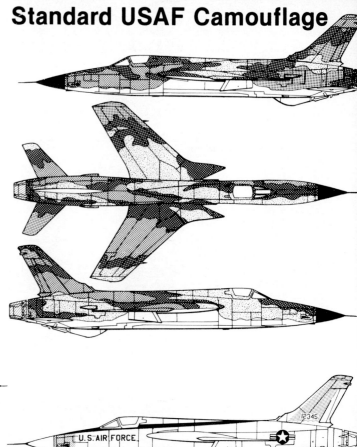

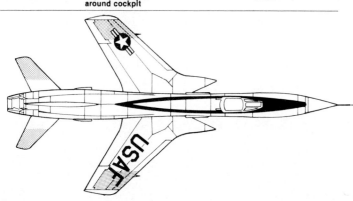

Those That Didn't Make It

It doesn't take a brilliant mathematician to realize that we have skipped a few digits in our Century Series coverage. So, what about those missing numbers? Was there an F-103, 107, 108, 109, 110? Yes, Virginia, there was, but none of them reached operational status with the exception of the **F-110**, which was really the F-4C. The Phantom II held the F-110 designation very briefly, probably only as a salve to Air Force pride for having to accept a Navy airplane. When DOD ruled that the same airplane could not hold different designations, it became the F-4C. I suppose a case could be made for including the F-111 in the Century Series, but it really did not gestate in the same period as the rest of them. It just doesn't seem like "one of the gang".

The one thing that those that did make it have in common with those that didn't is the fact that they were all born as a result of the tremendous explosion of aviation knowledge, and resulting design confidence, to come out of World War II. Some of those that didn't make it were cancelled because their designers were reaching just a little too much for their time. The **XF-103** is a case in point.

The XF-103 was conceived as a result of an Air Force request for proposals, embodied in MX-1554, "the 1954 interceptor". This request came about as a result of the research done in project MX-1187, which was an analysis of air defense capabilities and needs. Republic submitted three designs for consideration. The XF-103 was the most radical of the three, employing a turbojet and ramjet engine and, theoretically, being capable of Mach 3. This was in 1951, two years before any Century Series fighter was to fly. It was perhaps too radical a concept for the Air Force to consider as an operational possibility within three years. For whatever the reason, the Convair F-102 won the design competition. But the Air Force was impressed enough with the 103 to continue funding development costs.

How radical was the XF-103? The photo atop this column will tell you something. It really looked more like a missile, or perhaps what is known today as an RPV. It was 74 feet long, 19 feet tall and its delta wings spanned 36 feet. It was to have been capable of Mach 3 at 60,000 feet, with a service ceiling of 70,000 feet. It would weigh in at 43,000 lbs. for takeoff. The least impressive thing about the 103 was its range. It really was a point defense interceptor, with a combat radius of only 375 miles. One of the most radical things about the 103 was its skin. It would have been the first aircraft largely constructed of titanium planned for production.

Republic realized that there were other barriers to conquer besides the sonic barrier. At Mach 3 the skin of any airplane is going to get awfully hot. The answer to this problem was titanium. But the use of titanium created its own problems. Titanium is hard to work with. So the 103 design team went off on one of many tangents in search of the answers to that problem. There were other problems, of course. The XF-103 was truly pioneering. The story of its development, through six long and hard years, is one of perseverance and dedication that was finally rewarded with cancellation of the project in August 1957. But lest anyone think that all the time and effort expended on the project was in vain, consider the following: The titanium alloy developed for the 103 was used in the wing box of the F-14, the missiles that Hughes had been working on for use by the 103 led to similar developments for the XB-70 and F-111 and, of course, the development of heat-resistant metals certainly helped the folks in the Lockheed Skunk Works get the YF-12 into the air. The problems and frontiers faced by the 103 were just too numerous for any one project to handle, given existing state of the air technology. Add to that the inevitable service politics, and it is not surprising that the remarkable 103 never flew.

The North American **F-107A** came the closest of all of those that didn't make it. Three F-107As were produced and their development and initial flight testing was so successful that only politics could have killed the project.

The 107 began life as a progression of the basic F-100. But as the 106 was too advanced to become another version of the 102, so the 107 was too advanced to be another F-100. One of the biggest advances of the day was in powerplants. The J-75 engine gave the 107 50% more thrust than any F-100. Tactical Air Command's requirement for an advanced engine inlet configuration of the F-107. As it evolved, it became more and more evident to North American that the 107 should be treated as a completely new design. Their decision to compete for a contract in response to the Air Force WS-306A weapons system specification ensured the 107 a life of its own. North American received a contract for nine preproduction test aircraft in August 1954. The contract was amended to include three aircraft only in January 1957. First flight of the 107 was made on September 10, 1956, with North American Test Pilot Bob Baker flying 55-5118.

The second and third F-107s made their maiden flights in November 1956 and February 1957 respectively. Phase I testing had been completed, practically without a hitch, by November 17, 1956. Phase II testing was launched immediately, but intramural politicking had already sealed the fate of the F-107A. Although it was an outstanding aircraft, capable of a wide range of mission profiles, there was one thing it could not do as well as its chief competition....the F-105. If you remember anything at all about the 'fifties, you remember the overwhelming publicity heaped upon SAC. Along with all of this publicity (99% favorable) went the big budgets so necessary to develop new systems and ensure SAC dominance in the USAF. TAC was literally fighting for its life. There was no glamor in conventional warfare, especially during and right after the Korean War. What TAC needed for its image was the capability to perform the nuclear mission. The F-105 had an internal bomb bay which would carry a nuke and the 105 would go real fast down low, under the enemy radar. It was bigger than a B-17, but was flown by one man. It was just what TAC needed leading in early 1957 to the decision to kill the F-107 program.

The **F-108** was a North American project whose beginning almost exactly coincided with cancellation of the F-107. Unlike the multi-mission F-107, the F-108 was conceived solely for escort of the XB-70 Valkyrie, another North American airplane that didn't quite make it into the operational inventory. The F-108 resembled the XB-70, in that it had a delta wing and canards. And it was big, with a proposed combat weight of over 73,000 pounds. It was to have been a Mach 3 airplane, with a 1,000 nm combat radius. The program was cancelled in 1959. In retrospect, the reasons for cancellation probably revolved around the super-secret YF-12, which was then being brought to fruition in the Skunk Works of Lockheed.

The **F-109** was a Joint Air Force/Navy/Bell Aircraft venture to design a Mach 2 V-Stol interceptor. It only reached the mockup stage before being cancelled.

F-106 Delta Dart

Though produced in fewer numbers than any of the other Century Series fighters, the F-106 could be considered the most successful. After all, it is a pure air defense machine whose capabilities have withstood the test of time. The basic F-106 airframe has proven adaptable to all the demands of a changing air defense environment, from sophisticated ECM to Dissimilar Air Combat Maneuvering.

It will be readily apparent to even the casual observer that the F-102 and the F-106 are closely related. In fact, the two were to have been developed concurrently, the 106 originally having been designated F-102B. The problems associated with the F-102 program are covered in that chapter, those problems eventually leading to the separation of the 102 and 106 programs. The F-102, initially planned as an interim step to the 106, assumed a priority that led to its being produced in three times the numbers of its more sophisticated offspring.

Delays in the F-106 program were caused by the J-75 engine and the revolutionary MA-1 fire control system, so that the first flight of the F-106 did not take place until December 1956. The first production airplane lacked most of the production avionics (which in the case of the MA-1, amounted to a whopping 2,800 lbs) but that first flight left no doubt that the 106 was not in the least lacking in performance. It attained an altitude of 57,000 feet and a speed of Mach 1.9! Bringing the F-106 up to operational status required another 2½ years of testing and modifications. The first completely operational F-106 squadron was the 498th FIS, stationed at Geiger Field near Spokane, Washington. The "Geiger Tigers" became operational with the Dart in May 1959. The Six had been proclaimed operational, but in the following year there were no less than 63 changes to the control system and 67 changes to the airframe!

Distinctive canted intakes are one of the principle differences between the 106 and the 102. Another major difference is the way the fuselage is area-ruled. The 102 area-rule was achieved by adding on "bumps" to the rear of the fuselage, while the 106 fuselage looks as though it was bred with the area-rule. (Shinichi Ohtaki)

The F-106 has overcome its early production problems and developed into the premier all-weather fighter-interceptor. Throughout its life the 106 has received numerous changes to the fire control system and avionics. Recent changes have included improved radar systems, solid state TACAN and UHF radio, a one piece bubble canopy, and modifications to include a 20mm Vulcan cannon and "snap shoot" gunsight. The addition of solid state components has eased maintenance and resulted in some weight savings in the "black boxes" of the "Six". Other significant changes to the Dart have included an infrared seeker system and various electronic countermeasures features to the radar.

Since the 1967 modification to permit aerial refueling of the 106, it has been deployed to Korea and Labrador in support of world wide air defense requirements. When the Dart got aerial refuelling capability, the ADC realized that 106 pilots would have to be prepared to take on potential enemy fighters as well as bombers. Accordingly, in the late '60s, a program to train 106 pilots in air combat tactics was instituted. The F-106 proved to have excellent capability as an air combat fighter. Its large wing and high thrust enabled the 106 to outperform almost any airplane in the operational inventory, until the new generation of fighters (F-14, F-15, F-16, F-18) came along. Air Combat Training pointed up the need for the 106 to mount a gun to back up its missiles, the Air Defense Weapons Center testing and approving a modification that allows 106s to mount a 20mm gun in the weapons bay.

(Below Left) The 16th F-106A as it appeared during the test program at Edwards AFB in 1958. Note the wing fences which eventually removed from all production 106s. (Sullivan)

Late production configuration, which included air-to-air refuelling door (on spine, above "S" in "USAF") and leading edge slot in place of wing fences. (USAF)

F-106B with the weapons bay doors open and one Falcon Weapons System Evaluator Missile extended. This missile is a dummy which will track the target and provide telemetry on the accuracy of the pilot's intercept and simulated firing. (USAF)

This 106 was operated by Air Force Systems Command for specail test situations. Note addition to leading edge of wing at root....which contains a piece of equipment that remains a mystery to us. Whatever it was, it was obviously effective, as the scoreboard under the cockpit attests to the effectiveness of this airplane in "killing" drones. (General Dynamics)

(Right) Delta Darts of the famed *Hat In The Ring* 94th Aero Squadron, here operating as the 94th FIS, some 43 years after Eddie Rickenbacker insured everlasting fame for the squadron. (USAF)

F-106A-100-CO of the 460th FIS, at McChord AFB, 1972. Markings are yellow-gold and black.

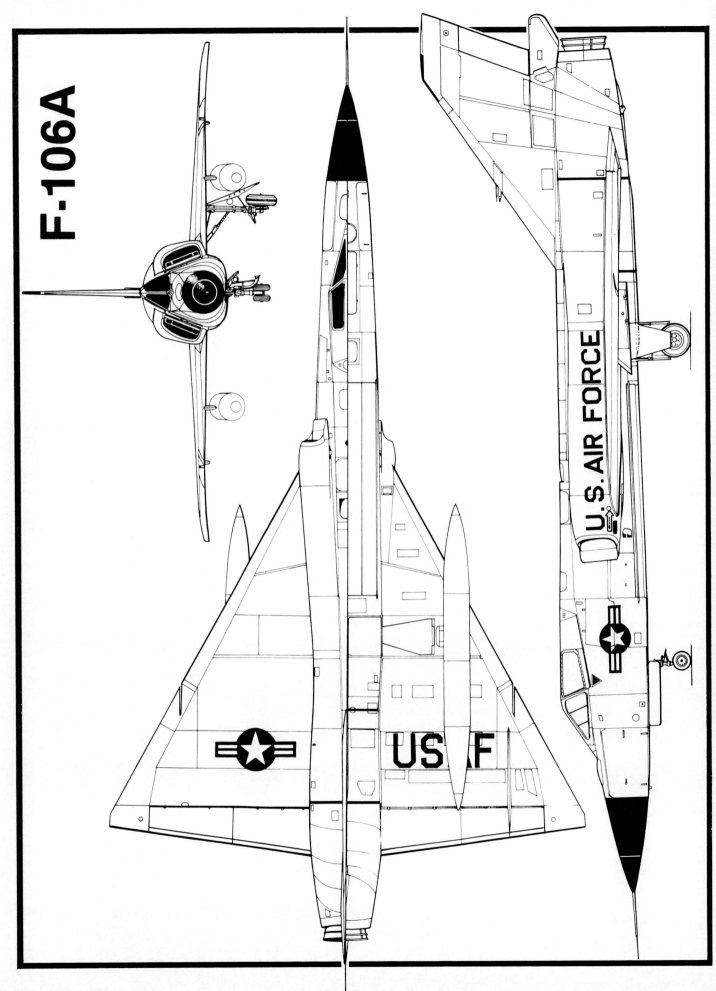

F-106A

U.S. AIR FORCE

USAF

F-106A-75-CO of the 465th FIS, 1963. Markings are yellow and black, with (from top) red, white, blue stripe at base of vertical fin.

(Above Right) F-106A-80-CO of the 539th FIS at L.G. Hanscom Field, Mass, October 1965. (Thomas S. Cuddy II via Paul Stevens)

F-106A-110-CO of the 27th FIS at Otis AFB, Mass, May 1965. Colors are yellow and black. Radome has recently been replaced and has yet to be painted. (Thomas S. Cuddy II via Paul Stevens)

F-106A-120-CO of the 49th FIS carried a message for the Army football team ("Beat Navy") on its wing tanks. At Nellis AFB, April 1972. (Peter Mancus via Jim Sullivan)

(Right and Above Right) F-106s of the 84th FIS carried colorful red/white/blue fin flashes and wing tank markings. They were based at Hamilton AFB, California in the early '70s. (Shinichi Ohtaki)

F-106A of the 48th FIS, Detachment 1, taking off from Wilmington, N.C. April 1970. The very noticeable hump in front of the cockpit is the housing for the retracted infra-red sensor. (Jim Sullivan)

(Below Left) Flight of four 106s of the 48th on initial for landing at Wilmington, N.C.,1970. The clean lines of the Six are most evident in plan view. It is not surprising that the speed record of 1,525mph set by the 106 in 1959 stood for nearly three years before falling to the mighty Phantom II. (Jim Sullivan)

Six of the 48th beginning his break for landing at Wilmington. (Sullivan)

Over the numbers at the end of the runway, the drag chute is beginning to deploy. (Sullivan)

Aerodynamic braking is employed in conjunction with the drag chute, as the Six keeps its nose high during rollout. (Sullivan)

Short runways require the techniques illustrated on the previous page plus heavy braking, leading to heavy wear on the tires. The F-106B made its first flight in April 1958. 63 were built. It differs from the A model only in the addition of the second seat, at the expense of internal fuel capacity. (Jim Sullivan)

The fertile mind and artistic talent of Captain Dick Stultz, of the 48th FIS were much in evidence at William Tell '78, as his creations graced several buildings. Stultz, formerly with the 87th FIS, was the creator of the memorable artwork carried by their 106s in the early '70s. "Taz" is the Tazlanglian Devil, personification of the 48th spirit, which trolls the Devil's Triangle in defense of the U.S. eastern shores. "Taz" is so mean he looks forward to being cornered! However, the U.S. Navy, represented by VF-21, was obviously not impressed, using one of their lances to strike a low blow at "Taz". (Paul Stevens)

Markings variations carried by the 11th FIS, later the 87th FIS. Seen in 1962 (above) with red and white stripes, blue chevron on the tail. In 1969 they carried a red delta with black outline (Above Right) Most recent marking reflects the Squadron name, the "Red Bulls". (Charles B. Mayer)

F-106A of the 120th Fighter Interceptor Group, Great Falls, Montana carries blue and white markings. It is one of five Air Guard units currently flying the 106. (via Paul Stevens)

F-106A of the 102nd Fighter Interceptor Wing, Otis AFB, MA

Six of the 144th Fighter Interceptor Wing, California Air Guard, as it appeared at William Tell '78, Tyndall AFB, Florida. Markings include a golden bear on a white tail, red at base of fin, with black lettering. (Paul Stevens)

F-106s of the 125th Fighter Interceptor Group, Jacksonville, Florida, Florida Air Guard. F-106 wing tanks are designed for supersonic flight, being in-flight refuellable or jettisonable. (Shinichi Ohtaki)

The clear-top canopy fitted to all 106s after 1972 is evident here, as is the immaculate finish of these Florida Air Guard 106s, which look as fresh as the day they left the factory. (Shinichi Ohtaki)

Variations on the markings carried by ADWC 106s. Early '70s scheme is illustrated above, while the current scheme is shown to the left. Colors in both are red, white and blue. 106 at top carries camera pods on underwing stations. Dual antennae under rear fuselage are for the data-link system. (Shinichi Ohtaki and USAF)

F-106 Aircraft Marking Specification

Standard USAF Camouflage

	MARKING	LOCATION	SIZE	FS COLOR NO.
A	U.S. AIR FORCE	Both side of fuselage	Letters 21" high	15044
B	Model Designation, Acft S/N and fuel Requirement	Left side of fuselage	Letters and numbers 1" high	17038
C	National Star	Both sides of fuselage	30" star	Background border - 15044, Stars and Bars - 17875, Stripes 11136
D		On under surface of right wing and top surface of left wing	40" star	
E	USAF	Top surface of right wing and under surface of left wing	30" high letters	15044
F	Call Numbers	Both sides of vertical stabilizer	12" high numbers	17038
G	Arctic Markings	One inch clearance around all large insignia and lettering		12197
H	Anti-Glare	Top of fuselage in front of cockpit		37038

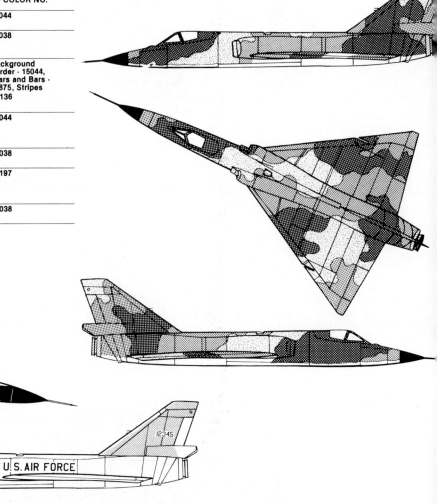